THE

# Paschal
# Mystery

# THE
# Paschal
# Mystery

### Reflections for Lent and Easter

Edited by Matthew Becklo

WORD
*on* FIRE.

Published by Word on Fire, Elk Grove Village, IL 60007
© 2023 by Word on Fire Catholic Ministries
Printed in the United States of America
All rights reserved

Cover design, typesetting, and interior art direction by Rozann Lee and Cassie Bielak

26 25 24 23    1 2 3 4

ISBN: 978-1-68578-031-9

Library of Congress Control Number: 2022910997

"Our paschal lamb,
Christ, has been sacrificed."

—1 CORINTHIANS 5:7

# Contents

# Introduction

Friends, thank you for joining us at Word on Fire for this journey through the Lenten and Easter seasons.

During Lent, we apprentice to Jesus in his forty-day sojourn in the desert. We stubbornly stay with him, doing what he did there, facing what he faced there. The desert is the place of clarification. When we have been stripped of the relatively trivial desires that preoccupy us, we can see, with a somewhat disturbing clarity, who we essentially are and what most pressingly matters.

Blaise Pascal said that most of us spend our lives seeking *divertissements* (distractions), for we cannot bear the weight of the great questions. We play, gossip, eat and drink, and seek the most banal entertainment so that we don't have to face the truth about ourselves, the reality of death, and the demands of God. The Spirit drives holy people into the desert because it is the place where the *divertissements* disappear: "He fasted forty days and forty nights" (Matt. 4:2). At the end of the Lord's fast, the tempter arrives—because decision follows clarification. How often in Scripture the theme of decision arises. Jesus himself provokes the stark choice: "Whoever is not with me is against me, and whoever does not gather with me scatters" (Matt. 12:30). And then Jesus is ready for mission; immediately after the temptations, he gathers his disciples around him and commences the ministry that will reach its culmination only on the cross.

So, this Lent, let us resolve to rid ourselves of *divertissements*, going a bit hungry and thirsty, purposely running on empty, so that the great questions may be asked with clarity. Let us get back to spiritual basics, focusing on Christ's suffering and uniting our own suffering—through fasting, prayer, and almsgiving—with the suffering members of the Church. Let us allow the devil to come, tempting us with the love of pleasure, power, and honor—for in temptation comes decision. Pleasure, power, and honor are in themselves good, but they are not the ultimate good; they are not God. "Worship the Lord your God, and serve only him" (Matt. 4:8). And in the desert with Jesus the Master, let us realize that we, too, are people on mission—because in decision comes identity.

This whole Lenten journey is meant to prepare us to embrace the Good News of Easter—the Resurrection of our Lord from the dead. In John's magnificent account of the Resurrection, he says that it was early in the morning on the first day of the week. It was still dark—just the way it was at the beginning of time before God said, "Let there be light" (Gen. 1:3). But a light was about to shine, and a new creation was about to appear. The stone had been rolled away. What was dreamed about, what endured as a hope against hope, has become a reality. God has opened the grave of his Son, and the bonds of death have been shattered forever. The Resurrection is the clearest indication of the lordship of Jesus. It is the fulcrum on which all of Christian faith turns. And it is a breakthrough even now in the midst of history of what God intends for his creation—both spiritual and material—at the end of time.

With our eyes fixed on this coming glory of Easter, let us together enter into this desert time of self-denial, ready to break out of the darkness of sin and death and into the light of the risen Christ.

Peace,

+ Robert Barron

Bishop Robert Barron

Ash Wednesday

# THE SHADOW
# OF DEATH

# Scripture

**Genesis 3:14–19**

Then the Lord God said to the serpent:
    "Because you have done this, you shall be banned
      from all the animals
      and from all the wild creatures;
    On your belly shall you crawl,
      and dirt shall you eat
      all the days of your life.
    I will put enmity between you and the woman,
      and between your offspring and hers;
    He will strike at your head,
      while you strike at his heel."
To the woman he said:
    "I will intensify the pangs of your childbearing;
      in pain shall you bring forth children.
    Yet your urge shall be for your husband,
      and he shall be your master."
To the man he said: "Because you listened to your wife and
ate from the tree of which I had forbidden you to eat,
    "Cursed be the ground because of you!
      In toil shall you eat its yield
      all the days of your life.
    Thorns and thistles shall it bring forth to you,
      as you eat of the plants of the field.

By the sweat of your face
  shall you get bread to eat,
Until you return to the ground,
  from which you were taken;
For you are dirt,
  and to dirt you shall return."

# Reading
**Bishop Barron**
**Homily**

Nothing in this world lasts. This is a truth about our world that is hard to take in, that has to be repeated to each generation afresh, and that many older people have an easier time understanding than young people. Everything in this world eventually fades away, evanesces, turns to dust. We hold everything here below temporarily. The Psalmist says, "You sweep them away; they are like a dream, like grass that is renewed in the morning; in the morning it flourishes and is renewed; in the evening it fades and withers. . . . Our years come to an end like a sigh" (Ps. 90:5–6, 9).

And listen to Qoheleth, the author of the book of Ecclesiastes: "Vanity of vanities! All is vanity" (Eccles. 1:2). They say that the sense of the Hebrew here is air or even "bubbles." Think of how fleeting, fragile, delicate a bubble is—and how quickly it breaks. So is the whole of life on earth.

Qoheleth invites us to consider a successful businessman who has labored and thought and planned very successfully over many years, accumulating a great fortune. At the end of the day, he has to give away everything he's worked so hard to attain. He takes none of it with him when he dies.

I might urge you to read the book of Ecclesiastes this week. You'll see an old man, usually identified as King Solomon, rehearsing all of the things he has done, all of the goods he has acquired—and finding all of it "a chasing after wind."

Now listen to Paul in his Letter to the Colossians: "If you have been raised with Christ, seek the things that are above, where Christ is, seated at the right hand of God. Set your minds on things that are above, not on things that are on earth" (Col. 3:1–2). We have here the same idea: things here below are passing, insubstantial, fleeting. Hence, our attention should be elsewhere—on the things that are above, that participate in the eternity of God.

Paul goes on: "Put to death, therefore, whatever in you is earthly: fornication, impurity, passion, evil desire, and greed (which is idolatry)" (Col. 3:5). Where do these things come from? They come from a preoccupation with wealth, pleasure, power, and honor—the goods of the world. Think about it: all of the violence, envy, warfare, and strife that we see every night on the news comes from a hyperconcern for

4

the passing goods here below.

In point of fact, that last word in Paul's quote gives away the game: "idolatry." This is nothing but the worship of what is less than God.

In the Gospels, Jesus tells the great parable of a rich man who has been so successful that he doesn't have space enough to store his harvest—and so he tears down his barns and builds bigger ones. So confident is he in his wealth that he says to himself, "You have ample goods laid up for many years; relax, eat, drink, be merry" (Luke 12:19). But that very night, he dies—and all of it comes to naught. "So it is with those who store up treasures for themselves but are not rich toward God" (Luke 12:21).

Here is something that St. Augustine said long ago: since every creature is made *ex nihilo*, it carries with it the heritage of nonbeing. There is a kind of penumbra or shadow of nothingness that haunts every finite thing. This is a rather high philosophical way of stating what all of us know in our bones. No matter how good, how beautiful a state of affairs is here below, it is destined to pass into nonbeing. That sunset that I enjoyed last night—that radiantly beautiful display—is now forever gone. It lasted only a while. That beautiful person—attractive, young, full of life, creative, joyful—will eventually age, get sick, break down, and die.

An image that always comes to mind when I think of these things is a gorgeous firework that bursts open like a

5

giant flower and then, in the twinkling of an eye, is gone forever. Everything is haunted by nonbeing. Everything, finally, is a firework.

But this is not meant to depress us; it is meant to redirect our attention precisely to the things that are "above," to the eternity of God.

# Reflection
## Pope St. John Paul II
## Homily

*"Return to the Lord, your God, for he is gracious and merciful"* (Joel 2:13).

With this exhortation taken from the book of the prophet Joel, the Church begins her Lenten pilgrimage, the acceptable time for returning: for returning to God from whom we have turned away. This, in fact, is the meaning of the penitential journey which starts today, Ash Wednesday: to return to the Father's house, bearing in our hearts the confession of our own guilt. The Psalmist invites us to say over and over: "Have mercy on me, O God, according to your steadfast love; according to your abundant mercy blot out my transgressions" (Ps. 51:1). With these sentiments, each of us sets out on the Lenten path, in the conviction that God the Father, who "sees in secret" (Matt. 6:4, 6, 18), goes out to meet the repentant sinner as he returns. As in the parable of the prodigal son, he embraces him and lets him understand that, by returning home, he has regained his dignity as a son: "he was dead, and is alive again; he was lost, and is found" (Luke 15:24). . . .

The very ancient and moving rite of ashes today opens this penitential journey. While putting ashes on the heads of the faithful, the celebrant warns each of them: *"Remember, you are dust and to dust you will return!"* (see Gen. 3:19).

These words also refer to a "return": the return to dust. They allude to the *necessity of death* and invite us not to forget that we are merely passing through this world.

At the same time, however, the expressive image of dust calls to mind the truth about creation with an allusion to the richness of the cosmic dimension of which the human creature forms a part. Lent recalls the work of salvation, to make man aware of the fact that death, a reality he must constantly face, is nevertheless not a *primordial truth*. Actually, it did not exist at the beginning, but, as the sad consequence of sin, it "entered the world through the devil's envy" (Wis. 2:24), becoming the common inheritance of human beings.

More than to other creatures, the words: *"Remember, you are dust and to dust you will return!"* are addressed to man, created by God in his own image and placed at the center of the universe. In reminding him that he must die, God does not abandon the initial plan, but rather confirms it and re-establishes it in an extraordinary way after the rupture

7

caused by original sin. This confirmation came to pass in Christ, who freely assumed the burden of sin and willingly submitted to death. The world thus became the scene of his saving Passion and death. This is the Paschal Mystery, to which the season of Lent directs us in a most special way.


## Prayer

**St. Francis of Assisi**
**"The Canticle of Brother Sun"**

Most High, all-powerful, good Lord,
Yours are the praises, the glory, the honor, and all blessing.
To You alone, Most High, do they belong,
and no man is worthy to mention Your name.
Praised be You, my Lord, with all your creatures,
especially Sir Brother Sun,
Who is the day and through whom You give us light.
And he is beautiful and radiant with great splendor;
and bears a likeness of You, Most High One.
Praised be You, my Lord, through Sister Moon and the stars,
in heaven You formed them clear and precious and
　　beautiful.
Praised be You, my Lord, through Brother Wind,
and through the air, cloudy and serene, and every kind of
　　weather

through which You give sustenance to Your creatures.
Praised be You, my Lord, through Sister Water,
which is very useful and humble and precious and chaste.
Praised be You, my Lord, through Brother Fire,
through whom You light the night
and he is beautiful and playful and robust and strong.
Praised be You, my Lord, through our Sister Mother Earth,
who sustains and governs us,
and who produces varied fruits with colored flowers and
    herbs.
Praised be You, my Lord, through those who give pardon
    for Your love
and bear infirmity and tribulation.
Blessed are those who endure in peace
for by You, Most High, they shall be crowned.
Praised be You, my Lord, through our Sister Bodily Death,
from whom no living man can escape.
Woe to those who die in mortal sin.
Blessed are those whom death will find in Your most holy
    will,
for the second death shall do them no harm.
Praise and bless my Lord and give Him thanks
and serve Him with great humility.
Amen.

# Hymn

*Dies Irae*

## Latin

*Dies irae, dies illa,*
*Solvet saeclum in favilla:*
*Teste David cum Sibylla.*

*Quantus tremor est futurus,*
*Quando Iudex est venturus,*
*Cuncta stricte discussurus!*

*Tuba, mirum spargens sonum*
*Per sepulcra regionum,*
*Coget omnes ante thronum.*

*Mors stupebit, et natura,*
*Cum resurget creatura,*
*Iudicanti responsura.*

*Liber scriptus proferetur,*
*In quo totum continetur,*
*Unde mundus iudicetur.*

## English

Day of wrath and doom impending,
David's word with Sibyl's blending,
Heaven and earth in ashes ending!

O, what fear man's bosom rendeth,
When from heaven the Judge descendeth,
On whose sentence all dependeth!

Wondrous sound the trumpet flingeth,
Through earth's sepulchres it ringeth,
All before the throne it bringeth.

Death is struck, and nature quaking,
All creation is awaking,
To its Judge an answer making.

Lo! the book exactly worded,
Wherein all hath been recorded;
Thence shall judgement be awarded.

*Iudex ergo cum sedebit,*
*Quidquid latet, apparebit:*
*Nil inultum remanebit.*

*Quid sum miser tunc dicturus?*
*Quem patronum rogaturus,*
*Cum vix iustus sit securus?*

*Rex tremendae maiestatis,*
*Qui salvandos salvas gratis,*
*Salva me, fons pietatis.*

*Recordare, Iesu pie,*
*Quod sum causa tuae viae:*
*Ne me perdas illa die.*

*Quaerens me, sedisti lassus:*
*Redemisti Crucem passus:*
*Tantus labor non sit cassus.*

*Iuste Iudex ultionis,*
*Donum fac remissionis*
*Ante diem rationis.*

When the Judge his seat attaineth,
And each hidden deed arraigneth,
Nothing unavenged remaineth.

What shall I, frail man, be pleading?
Who for me be interceding,
When the just are mercy needing?

King of majesty tremendous,
Who doest free salvation send us,
Fount of pity, then befriend us!

Think, kind Jesus! — my salvation
Caused thy wondrous Incarnation;
Leave me not to reprobation.

Faint and weary thou hast sought me,
On the cross of suffering bought me;
Shall such grace be vainly brought me?

Righteous Judge! for sin's pollution
Grant thy gift of absolution,
Ere that day of retribution.

*Ingemisco, tamquam reus:*
*Culpa rubet vultus meus:*
*Supplicanti parce, Deus.*

*Qui Mariam absolvisti,*
*Et latronem exaudisti,*
*Mihi quoque spem dedisti.*

*Preces meae non sunt dignae:*
*Sed tu bonus fac benigne,*
*Ne perenni cremer igne.*

*Inter oves locum praesta,*
*Et ab haedis me sequestra,*
*Statuens in parte dextra.*

*Confutatis maledictis,*
*Flammis acribus addictis,*
*Voca me cum benedictis.*

*Oro supplex et acclinis,*
*Cor contritum quasi cinis:*
*Gere curam mei finis.*

Guilty, now I pour my moaning,
All my shame with anguish owning;
Spare, O God, thy suppliant groaning!

Through the sinful woman shriven,
Through the dying thief forgiven,
Thou to me a hope hast given.

Worthless are my prayers and sighing,
Yet, good Lord, in grace complying,
Rescue me from fires undying.

With thy sheep a place provide me,
From the goats afar divide me,
To thy right hand do thou guide me.

When the wicked are confounded,
Doomed to shame and woe unbounded,
Call me, with thy saints surrounded.

Low I kneel, with heart's submission,
See, like ashes my contrition!
Help me in my last condition!

*Lacrimosa dies illa,*
*Qua resurget ex favilla*
*Iudicandus homo reus:*
*Huic ergo parce, Deus.*

*Pie Iesu Domine,*
*Dona eis requiem. Amen.*

Ah! that day of tears and mourning!
From the dust of earth returning,
Man for judgment must prepare him:
Spare, O God, in mercy spare him!

Lord, all-pitying, Jesus blest,
Grant them thine eternal rest. Amen.

# Reflection

**Second Vatican Council**
*Gaudium et Spes*

It is in the face of death that the riddle of human existence grows most acute. Not only is man tormented by pain and by the advancing deterioration of his body, but even more so by a dread of perpetual extinction. He rightly follows the intuition of his heart when he abhors and repudiates the utter ruin and total disappearance of his own person. He rebels against death because he bears in himself an eternal seed which cannot be reduced to sheer matter. All the endeavors of technology, though useful in the extreme, cannot calm his anxiety; for prolongation of biological life is unable to satisfy that desire for higher life which is inescapably lodged in his breast.

Although the mystery of death utterly beggars the imagination, the Church has been taught by divine revelation and firmly teaches that man has been created by God for a blissful purpose beyond the reach of earthly misery. In addition, that bodily death from which man would have been immune had he not sinned will be vanquished, according to the Christian faith, when man who was ruined by his own doing is restored to wholeness by an almighty and merciful Savior. For God has called man and still calls him so that with his entire being he might be joined to him in an endless sharing of a divine life beyond all corruption. Christ won this victory when he rose to life, for by his death he freed man from death. Hence to every thoughtful man a solidly established faith provides the answer to his anxiety about what the future holds for him. At the same time faith gives him the power to be united in Christ with his loved ones who have already been snatched away by death; faith arouses the hope that they have found true life with God.

# Poem

**Gerard Manley Hopkins**
**"Spring and Fall"**

*To a young child*

Márgarét, áre you grieving
Over Goldengrove unleaving?
Leáves, líke the things of man, you
With your fresh thoughts care for, can you?
Áh! ás the heart grows older
It will come to such sights colder
By and by, nor spare a sigh
Though worlds of wanwood leafmeal lie;
And yet you wíll weep and know why.
Now no matter, child, the name:
Sórrow's spríngs áre the same.
Nor mouth had, no nor mind, expressed
What heart heard of, ghost guessed:
It is the blight man was born for,
It is Margaret you mourn for.

# Prayer

**St. Thérèse of Lisieux**
*Story of a Soul* **Epilogue (Her Last Words)**

My God, I love you!

"For the wages of sin is death, but the free gift of God is eternal life in Christ Jesus our Lord."

—ROMANS 6:23

# The First
# Week *of* Lent

# INTO THE DESERT

**Mark 1:1–13**

The beginning of the gospel of Jesus Christ the Son of God. As it is written in Isaiah the prophet:

*Behold, I am sending my messenger ahead of you;*
*he will prepare your way.*
*A voice of one crying out in the desert:*
*"Prepare the way of the Lord,*
*make straight his paths."*

John the Baptist appeared in the desert proclaiming a baptism of repentance for the forgiveness of sins. People of the whole Judean countryside and all the inhabitants of Jerusalem were going out to him and were being baptized by him in the Jordan River as they acknowledged their sins. John was clothed in camel's hair, with a leather belt around his waist. He fed on locusts and wild honey. And this is what he proclaimed: "One mightier than I is coming after me. I am not worthy to stoop and loosen the thongs of his sandals. I have baptized you with water; he will baptize you with the Holy Spirit."

It happened in those days that Jesus came from Nazareth of Galilee and was baptized in the Jordan by John. On coming up out of the water he saw the heavens being torn open and the Spirit, like a dove, descending upon him. And a voice came from the heavens, "You are my beloved Son; with you I am well pleased."

The Spirit drove Jesus out into the desert, and he remained in the desert for forty days, tempted by Satan. He was among wild beasts, and the angels ministered to him.

# Reading

**Bishop Barron**
*The Great Story of Israel*

The holy season of Lent arises from Jesus' forty days in the desert. The number forty—a classical biblical number, from the flood lasting forty days and forty nights to the Israelites wandering in the desert for forty years—signals the mystical and religious purpose of this enterprise. The Lord, who enters fully into our human condition without becoming a sinner, nonetheless wrestles with all the temptations that we wrestle with. He is "one who in every respect has been tested as we are, yet without sin" (Heb. 4:15). Very early on in the life of the Church, Christians recognized that if the Lord went into the desert, then we ought to go into it too; we, too, need to fast and to face down our demons. Thus, Lent is fundamentally an *imitatio Christi* (imitation of Christ).

The desert is a place of simplicity and poverty, a place where illusions die, where reality is faced honestly and without compromise. But the desert also symbolizes the spiritual space of sin. At the beginning of the Bible, we read of the expulsion from the Garden of Eden. God's purpose for us is the garden, which signals life, and life to the full. The Church Fathers see the garden as all forms of human flourishing, including science, philosophy, and friendship.

After the fall, Adam and Eve are cast out of the garden—not because God is being petulant, but because sin is by its very nature this expulsion. Sin creates a desert experience. We see this reflected in Michelangelo's Sistine Chapel ceiling: Adam and Eve are depicted in the sumptuous space of the garden, but after the fall, we see them being driven out into a completely barren, desert-like environment, symbolizing sin and the effects of sin. This is part of why so many of the great heroes of Israel—Abraham, Isaac, Jacob, Moses, the prophets—have to spend time in the desert: they have to get in touch with their own sinfulness, to purge away what needs purging.

Moses, the prince of Egypt, is raised in a sumptuous, powerful environment, but is beset by his own sins. Seeing an Egyptian beating a Hebrew, Moses kills the aggressor and quickly buries him in the sand. A few days later, he attempts to intervene in an argument between two Hebrews and is sharply rebuked: "Who made you a ruler and judge over us? Do you mean to kill me as you killed the Egyptian?" (Exod. 2:14). Understanding that his murder has become widely known, he immediately flees the country. So what do we know of Moses? He is clearly a man of moral principle but also more than a little imperious, self-important, judgmental, rash, and violent. In time, he will become the liberator of his people, but at this point in the narrative, he is full of potential, but also full of himself, and not ready for the kind of leadership that God wants him to exercise. A time of trial and testing will be required, and as is so often the case in the Bible, this will take place in the desert.

Another example is found in the beautifully told and psychologically profound story of Joseph in the book of Genesis. Since he was the child of his father's old age, Joseph was the particular favorite of Jacob, who gifted the boy with a lovely, long-sleeved robe, probably hinting at something like royal status. Naturally, his brothers hated him. Making matters worse, Joseph was a dreamer who never hesitated to share his dreams with his family. And making matters worse still, no Freudian feats of dream interpretation were required to understand that these nighttime fantasies served to aggrandize Joseph's ego. In one, he and his brothers were binding sheaves, when suddenly Joseph's stood upright and those of his brothers bowed down in homage; in another, the sun, moon, and stars—the cosmic elements themselves—paid homage to Joseph. His brothers, of course, hate him, and send him, as it were, into the desert. They strip him of his special coat and throw him into a pit. At Judah's suggestion, they don't kill the boy, but rather arrange for his sale to a passing caravan of Ishmaelite traders on their way to Egypt. Icarus-like, Joseph, who had certainly been flying too high, is now cast down—down into the pit and then "down" into Egypt, where, after being falsely accused by the wife of Potiphar, he is compelled to spend several years in prison.

It was precisely the long period of confinement, rejection, and deep suffering that worked an alchemy in his soul and prepared him for the task at hand.

In the season of Lent, we get in touch with our own sin, with what has produced a desert in us. We don't cover it up, make excuses for it, or dull our sensitivity to it; rather, following Jesus, we face down our own fears and temptations in the desert.

# Reflection

**St. Athanasius**
*Life of St. Anthony*

He was alone in the inner mountain, spending his time in prayer and discipline. And the brethren who served him asked that they might come every month and bring him olives, pulse, and oil, for by now he was an old man. There then he passed his life, and endured such great wrestlings, "not against flesh and blood" (Eph. 6:12), as it is written, but against opposing demons, as we learned from those who visited him. For there they heard tumults, many voices, and, as it were, the clash of arms. At night they saw the mountain become full of wild beasts, and him also fighting as though against visible beings, and praying against them. And those who came to him he encouraged, while kneeling he contended and prayed to the Lord. Surely it was a marvelous thing that a man, alone in such a desert, feared neither the demons who rose up against him, nor the fierceness of the four-footed beasts and creeping things, for they were numerous. But in truth, as it is written, "he trusted in the Lord as Mount Zion" (see Ps. 125:1), with a mind unshaken and undisturbed; so that the demons rather fled from him, and the wild beasts, as it is written, "kept peace with him" (Job 5:23).

# Prayer

**Desert Hermit**

*The Desert Fathers: Sayings of the Early Christian Monks*

Lord, you have mercy even on the wicked, even the pitiless; you commanded us to show mercy to our neighbors; therefore have mercy upon me, humbled here before you. With you nothing is impossible, for at the mouth of hell my soul was scattered like dust. Have pity on what you have made because you are good and merciful; on the day of the resurrection you will raise up even the bodies of those who are not. Hear me, O Lord, for my spirit has failed, and my soul is wretched. . . .

Look at my penitence and forgive my sin. . . . Send life into me, for I am contrite . . . so I may be able to have confidence in your mercy and forgiveness, and so keep your commandments, remain in awe of you, and serve you more faithfully than before, for the rest of the life which you have given me.

Amen.

# Hymn

*Antra Deserti*

**Latin**

*Antra deserti, teneris sub annis,*
*Civium turmas fugiens, petisti,*
*Ne levi posses maculare vitam*
*Crimine linguae.*

*Praebuit durum tegumen camelus*
*Artubus sacris, strophium bidentes;*
*Cui latex haustum, sociata pastum*
*Mella locustis.*

*Caeteri tantum cecinere Vatum*
*Corde praesago iubar affuturum:*
*Tu quidem mundi scelus auferentem*
*Indice prodis.*

*Non fuit vasti spatium per orbis*
*Sanctior quisquam genitus Ioanne,*
*Qui nefas saecli meruit lavantem*
*Tingere lymphis.*

**English**

Thou, in thy childhood, to the desert caverns
Fleddest for refuge from the cities' turmoil,
Where the world's slander might not dim thy luster,
Lonely abiding.

Camel's hair raiment clothed thy saintly members;
Leathern the girdle which thy loins encircled;
Locusts and honey, with the fountain-water,
Daily sustained thee.

Oft in past ages, seers with hearts expectant
Sang the far-distant advent of the Day-Star;
Thine was the glory, as the world's Redeemer
First to proclaim him.

Far as the wide world reacheth, born of woman,
Holier was there none than John the Baptist;
Meetly in water laving him who cleanseth
Man from pollution.

*Sit decus Patri, genitaeque Proli,*
*Et tibi, compar utriusque virtus*
*Spiritus semper, Deus unus, omni*
*Temporis aevo.*

Praise to the Father, to the Son begotten,
And to the Spirit, equal power possessing,
One God whose glory, through the lapse of ages,
Ever resoundeth.

# Reflection

**Thomas Merton**
*The Wisdom of the Desert*

The simple men who lived their lives out to a good old age among the rocks and sands only did so because they had come into the desert to be themselves, their *ordinary* selves, and to forget a world that divided them from themselves. There can be no other valid reason for seeking solitude or for leaving the world. And thus to leave the world, is, in fact, to help save it in saving oneself. . . . The Coptic hermits who left the world as though escaping from a wreck, did not merely intend to save themselves. They knew that they were helpless to do any good for others as long as they floundered about in the wreckage. But once they got a foothold on solid ground, things were different. Then they had not only the power but even the obligation to pull the whole world to safety after them.

This is their paradoxical lesson for our time. It would perhaps be too much to say that the world needs another movement such as that which drew these men into the deserts of Egypt and Palestine. Ours is certainly a time for solitaries and for hermits. But merely to reproduce the simplicity, austerity, and prayer of these primitive souls is not a complete or satisfactory answer. We must transcend them, and transcend all those who, since their time, have gone beyond the limits which they set. We must liberate ourselves, in our own way, from involvement in a world that is plunging to disaster. But our world is different from theirs. Our involvement in it is more complete. Our danger is far more desperate. Our time, perhaps, is shorter than we think.

We cannot do exactly what they did. But we must be as thorough and as ruthless in our determination to break all spiritual chains, and cast off the domination of alien compulsions, to find our true selves, to discover and develop our inalienable spiritual liberty and use it to build, on earth, the kingdom of God.

# Poem

**Thomas Merton**
**From "St. John Baptist"**

*What did you learn on the wild mountain*
*When hell came dancing on the noon-day rocks?*

"I learned my hands could hold
Rivers of water
And spend them like an everlasting treasure.
I learned to see the waking desert
Smiling to behold me with the springs her ransom,
Open her clear eyes in a miracle of transformation,
And the dry wilderness
Suddenly dressed in meadows,
All garlanded with an embroidery of flowering orchards
Sang with a virgin's voice,
Descending to her wedding in these waters
With the Prince of Life.
All barrenness and death lie drowned
Here in the fountains He has sanctified,
And the deep harps of Jordan
Play to the contrite world as sweet as heaven."

# Prayer

**St. Thérèse of Lisieux**
**From "My Song for Today"**

Lord, let me hide in your Face,
There I'll no longer hear the world's vain noise.
Give me your love, keep me in your grace
    Just for today.

Near your divine Heart, I forget all passing things,
I no longer dread the fears of the night.
Jesus, give me a place in your Heart
    Just for today.

Living Bread, Bread of Heaven, divine Eucharist,
O sacred Mystery! that Love has brought forth. . . .
Come live in my heart, Jesus, my white Host,
    Just for today.

Amen.

"The contemplatives and ascetics of all ages and religions have sought God in the silence and solitude of the desert, forest, and mountains. Jesus himself spent forty days in the desert and the mountains, communing for long hours with the Father in the silence of the night. We too are called to withdraw at certain intervals into deeper silence and aloneness with God."

—ST. TERESA OF KOLKATA

# The Second
# Week *of* Lent

# PRAYER, FASTING,
# ALMSGIVING

# Scripture
## Matthew 6:1–18

Jesus said to his disciples: "Take care not to perform righteous deeds in order that people may see them; otherwise, you will have no recompense from your heavenly Father. When you give alms, do not blow a trumpet before you, as the hypocrites do in the synagogues and in the streets to win the praise of others. Amen, I say to you, they have received their reward. But when you give alms, do not let your left hand know what your right is doing, so that your almsgiving may be secret. And your Father who sees in secret will repay you.

"When you pray, do not be like the hypocrites, who love to stand and pray in the synagogues and on street corners so that others may see them. Amen, I say to you, they have received their reward. But when you pray, go to your inner room, close the door, and pray to your Father in secret. And your Father who sees in secret will repay you.

"In praying, do not babble like the pagans, who think that they will be heard because of their many words. Do not be like them. Your Father knows what you need before you ask him.

"This is how you are to pray:
Our Father who art in heaven,
    hallowed be thy name,

    thy Kingdom come,
thy will be done,
    on earth as it is in heaven.
Give us this day our daily bread;
and forgive us our trespasses,
    as we forgive those who trespass against us;
and lead us not into temptation,
    but deliver us from evil.

"If you forgive men their transgressions, your heavenly Father will forgive you. But if you do not forgive men, neither will your Father forgive your transgressions.

"When you fast, do not look gloomy like the hypocrites. They neglect their appearance, so that they may appear to others to be fasting. Amen, I say to you, they have received their reward. But when you fast, anoint your head and wash your face, so that you may not appear to be fasting, except to your Father who is hidden. And your Father who sees what is hidden will repay you."

# Reading

**Bishop Barron**
*The Strangest Way*

During the privileged time of Lent, the Church recommends to us three activities, three things to *do*: prayer, fasting, and almsgiving.

First, prayer. Christian prayer is an embodied business. In C.S. Lewis' *Screwtape Letters*, one of the recommendations that the training devil gives to his young charge is to encourage his "client" to think that prayer is something very "interior" and "mystical," having little to do with posture or the position of the body. He wants the poor man to think that whether one stands, slouches, sits, or kneels is irrelevant to the quality of one's communication with God.

But the centrality of gesture, posture, and movement in the act of prayer has long been taken for granted in the Christian tradition. Thus, in the Hesychast movement in Eastern Christianity, great stress is placed upon the act of breathing while reciting the mantra-like "Jesus Prayer." This is an adaptation of the words of the publican in Jesus' parable: "Lord Jesus Christ, Son of God, have mercy on me, a sinner." While one prays the first part of the mantra, one is encouraged to breathe in deeply, filling the lungs entirely. This act symbolizes the filling of the heart with the living presence of Christ, the placing of Jesus at the center of all that we are. At the conclusion of this first part of the prayer, one holds one's breath for a brief period and then exhales while reciting the conclusion: "Have mercy on me, a sinner." This last gesture evokes the expelling of sin from the heart. The double movement—breathing in and breathing out—is thus a sort of cleansing process, a taking in of the Holy Spirit and a letting go of unclean spirits. The prayer (and the feel of it in one's lungs and body) can become second nature, automatic, a constant accompaniment of one's activity and inactivity. My grandmother used to pray the Jesus Prayer in this way, breathing it out almost inaudibly whenever she sat down. However it is practiced, it is a vivid way of reminding the body of the center.

Another intensely bodily (though much-maligned) practice of prayer is the Rosary. For me, the most striking quality of praying the Rosary is its deliberate pace, the way it, despite ourselves, slows us down. Like the Jesus Prayer, the Rosary is a mantra—that is to say, a prayer of almost hypnotic repetition. Masters in the Buddhist tradition of meditation speak of "calming the monkey mind." This means the settling of the superficial mind that dances and darts from preoccupation to preoccupation and whose concerns tend to dominate our consciousness: "What is my next appointment? Where do I go next? What did she mean by that?" In order to open up the deepest ground of the soul—the center—that mind must be, at least for a time, quelled. In the Rosary meditation, the mantra of the repeated Hail Marys quiets the monkey mind, compelling it to cede place to deeper reaches of the psyche.

Second, fasting. The appetites for food and drink are so pressing, so elemental, that unless they are quelled and disciplined, they will simply take over the soul. They are like children who clamor constantly for attention and who, if indulged, will in short order run the house. Therefore, if the desire for the center, the passion for God, be awakened, the more immediately pressing desires must be muted, and this is the purpose of fasting in its various forms. We force ourselves to go hungry so that the deepest hunger might be felt and fed; we force ourselves to go thirsty so that the profoundest thirst might be sensed and quenched. In a way, fasting is like the "calming of the monkey mind" effected by the Rosary prayer: both are means of stilling the effervescence of relatively superficial preoccupations.

For years, one of the best-known practices in the Catholic tradition was the Friday abstinence from meat throughout the year. By this modest act of self-denial, Catholics identified themselves with the sufferings of Christ on Good Friday, signaling with their bodily behavior a focus upon the center. But another advantage of this practice—often overlooked—was the social bond and corporate sensibility that it created among Catholics; it was a public act that identified them as a unique social group, establishing a clear line of demarcation between themselves and others. Now, there is no question that the importance of this gesture became, in some cases, exaggerated (eat meat on Friday and go directly to hell), and, with the exception of Lent, it was accordingly muted in the period after Vatican II, becoming first a voluntary, self-imposed discipline and then passing largely into oblivion. But in the suspension of abstinence laws, the capacity of the Catholic community to define itself and to speak a challenging word to the culture—even in a simple way—was seriously compromised.

Finally, almsgiving. A kind of fasting from money and what it can buy is an important practice of the Christian community. How often in the Gospels Jesus recommends that his disciples sell all they have or abandon everything or give to the poor, and how often throughout the Christian tradition has the discipline of almsgiving been emphasized. In the Acts of the Apostles, we hear that the earliest community of believers sold their belongings and laid the proceeds at the feet of the Apostles for equitable distribution (Acts 4:35).

So how does a community behave who find their security not in wealth but in Jesus Christ? They could embrace the ancient biblical practice of tithing, giving 10 percent of their income to the poor or to the Church. They could place in their homes, right by the door, an alms box, and each time they leave, they could put something in it for those who have little. They could set an extra place at their family table, and they could give what they would have spent on that meal to the brother or sister who does not have enough to eat. They could go into their probably overstuffed closets on a regular basis and take out shirts, pants, and dresses for those who need them. (St. Ambrose said that if the Christian has two shirts in his closet, one belongs to him, and the other belongs to the man with no shirt. And Pope Leo XIII, in his social encyclical *Rerum Novarum,* stated that once the demands of necessity and propriety are met, everything that a person owns should be directed to the common good.) Or they could find the car, home, or television that they want and could afford and then purposely buy a less expensive model, giving the difference to the poor. Or, realizing that concern for the homeless and the hungry in their community is not an abstract "social problem," but rather the concrete responsibility of Christians, they could directly spend their wealth to feed and house those in need.

And so, we resist Screwtape's suggestion that we spiritualize our faith. And we center ourselves in Christ with the whole self—praying, breathing, fingering beads, fasting, and almsgiving our way along the path of holiness.

# Reflection

**St. Augustine**

**Sermon**

By the help of the merciful Lord our God, the temptations of the world, the snares of the Devil, the suffering of the world, the enticement of the flesh, the surging waves of troubled times, and all corporal and spiritual adversities are to be overcome by almsgiving, fasting, and prayer. These practices ought to glow throughout the entire life of a Christian, but especially as the Paschal solemnity approaches which stirs up our minds by its yearly return, renewing in them the salutary memory that our Lord, the only-begotten Son of God, showed mercy to us and fasted and prayed for us. . . .

In regard to almsgiving, we are commanded to give bread to the hungry (see Isa. 58:7), but he first gave himself over to cruel enemies for us so that he might give himself as food to us when we were hungry. . . . Let us give alms the more generously and the more frequently in proportion as the day draws nearer on which the supreme almsgiving accomplished for us is celebrated. Fasting without mercy is worthless to him who fasts.

Let us fast, humbling our souls as the day draws near on which the Teacher of humility humbled himself becoming obedient even to death on a cross (see Phil. 2:8). Let us imitate his cross, fastening to it our passions subdued by the nails of abstinence. Let us chastise our body, subjecting it to obedience, and, lest we slip into illicit pleasures through our undisciplined flesh, let us in taming it sometimes withdraw licit pleasures. . . .

During these days of Lent our prayer is lifted up to God, supported by pious almsgiving and by tempered fasting. . . . Surely, just as we are rendered fit for praying by almsgiving and fasting, so our prayer itself gives alms when it is directed and poured forth not only for friends but for enemies as well and when it refrains from anger, hatred, and harmful vices. For, if we fast from food, how much more does prayer recoil from poisons? Finally, while we are refreshed by taking food at regular and suitable times, let us never distract our prayer by such feasts. Rather let it endure perpetual fasts because there is a food proper to prayer which it is commanded to take without ceasing. Therefore, let it always fast from hatred and feast upon love.

# Prayer

**Dorothy Day**
*The Duty of Delight*

Dear God, forgive me, my failures, my lack of prayer. I have not begun to learn how. You will have to teach me, draw me, and I will run after the odor of your garments. . . .

My very weakness, I will try not to worry so much about. I accept my backaches, headaches, torment of mind as penance for my sins.

Help me to be patient.

Amen.

# Hymn

*Audi Benigne Conditor*

**Latin**

*Audi benigne Conditor*
*Nostras preces cum fle tibus,*
*In hoc sacro ieiunio*
*Fusas quadragenario.*

*Scrutator alme cordium,*
*Infirma tu scis virium:*
*Ad te reversis exhibe*
*Remissionis gratiam.*

*Multum quidem peccavimus,*
*Sed parce confitentibus:*
*Ad nominis laudem tui*
*Confer medelam languidis.*

*Concede nostrum conteri*
*Corpus per abstinentiam;*
*Culpae ut relinquant pabulum*
*Ieiuna corda criminum.*

## English

O kind Creator, bow thine ear
To mark the cry, to know the tear
Before thy throne of mercy spent
In this thy holy fast of Lent.

Our hearts are open, Lord, to thee:
Thou knowest our infirmity;
Pour out on all who seek thy face
Abundance of thy pardoning grace.

Our sins are many, this we know;
Spare us, good Lord, thy mercy show;
And for the honor of thy name
Our fainting souls to life reclaim.

Give us the self-control that springs
From discipline of outward things,
That fasting inward secretly
The soul may purely dwell with thee.

*Praesta, beata Trinitas,*
*Concede simplex Unitas;*
*Ut fructuosa sint tuis*
*Ieiuniorum munera.*

We pray thee, Holy Trinity,
One God, unchanging Unity,
That we from this our abstinence
May reap the fruits of penitence.

# Reflection

**St. Cyprian**
*On Works and Alms*

He shall not be able to deserve the mercy of the Lord, who himself shall not have been merciful; nor shall he obtain anything from the divine pity in his prayers, who shall not have been humane towards the poor man's prayer. And this also the Holy Spirit declares in the Psalms, and proves, saying, "Blessed is he that considers of the poor and needy; the Lord will deliver him in the evil day" (Ps. 41:1). . . .

Raphael the angel also witnesses the like, and exhorts that alms should be freely and liberally bestowed, saying, "Prayer is good, with fasting and alms; because alms deliver from death, and it purges away sins" (Tob. 12:8–9). He shows that our prayers and fastings are of less avail, unless they are aided by almsgiving; that entreaties alone are of little force to obtain what they seek, unless they be made sufficient by the addition of deeds and good works. The angel reveals, and manifests, and certifies that our petitions become efficacious by almsgiving, that life is redeemed from dangers by almsgiving, that souls are delivered from death by almsgiving.

# Poem

**Gerard Manley Hopkins**
**"The Starlight Night"**


Look at the stars! Look, look up at the skies!
    O look at all the fire-folk sitting in the air!
    The bright boroughs, the circle-citadels there!
Down in dim woods the diamond delves! The elves'-eyes!
The grey lawns cold where gold, where quickgold lies!
    Wind-beat whitebeam! Airy abeles set on a flare!
    Flake-doves sent floating forth at a farmyard scare!—
Ah well! It is all a purchase, all is a prize.

Buy then! bid then!—What?—Prayer, patience, alms, vows.
Look, look: a May-mess, like on orchard boughs!
    Look! March-bloom, like on mealed-with-yellow sallows!
These are indeed the barn; withindoors house
The shocks. This piece-bright paling shuts the spouse
    Christ home, Christ and his mother and all his hallows.

# Prayer

**St. Thérèse of Lisieux**
**Morning Offering**

My God, I offer you all that I do today for the intentions and the glory of the Sacred Heart of Jesus. I want to sanctify every beat of my heart, my thoughts, and my simplest works by uniting them to his infinite merits. I want to repair for my faults by casting them into the furnace of his merciful love.

O my God! I ask you for myself and those dear to me the grace to fulfill perfectly your holy will and to accept for love of you the joys and sorrows of this passing life so that one day we may be reunited in heaven for all eternity.

Amen.

"In prayer faith remains steadfast, in fastings life remains innocent, in almsgiving the mind remains kind."

—POPE ST. LEO THE GREAT

# The Third
# Week *of* Lent

# TEMPTATION

# Scripture
## Matthew 4:1–11

At that time Jesus was led by the Spirit into the desert to be tempted by the devil. He fasted for forty days and forty nights, and afterwards he was hungry. The tempter approached and said to him, "If you are the Son of God, command that these stones become loaves of bread." He said in reply, "It is written:

*One does not live by bread alone,*
 *but on every word that comes forth*
  *from the mouth of God."*

Then the devil took him to the holy city, and made him stand on the parapet of the temple, and said to him, "If you are the Son of God, throw yourself down. For it is written:

*He will command his angels concerning you*
 *and with their hands they will support you,*
  *lest you dash your foot against a stone."*

Jesus answered him, "Again it is written,

*You shall not put the Lord, your God, to the test."*

Then the devil took him up to a very high mountain, and showed him all the kingdoms of the world in their magnificence, and he said to him, "All these I shall give to you, if you will prostrate yourself and worship me." At this, Jesus said to him, "Get away, Satan! It is written:

*The Lord, your God, shall you worship*
*and him alone shall you serve."*

Then the devil left him and, behold, angels came and ministered to him.

# Reading
**Bishop Barron**
*The Priority of Christ*

At the limits of his endurance, Jesus confronts the enemy: "The tempter came and said to him, 'If you are the Son of God, command these stones to become loaves of bread'" (Matt. 4:3). The devil's conditional clause—"if you are the Son of God"—reveals that what is at stake in this struggle is the nature of Jesus' messiahship. Throughout Israelite history, the Messiah's office had been imagined in a variety of ways: liberator, eschatological prophet, suffering servant. In the measure that Jesus realizes true Christhood, he will be able to outmaneuver his opponent; in the measure that the scatterer can lure Jesus into a false conception of his mission, he will carry the day.

This first temptation is low level, symbolized by the desert floor strewn with stones. It is the attempt to move Jesus away from the will and purposes of God through a crude appeal to his animal instincts. Hunger for food is spiritually equivalent to the desire for sexual pleasure and sensual delight, for the satisfaction of the most immediate needs of the body. Precisely because they are immediate and insistent, these desires can easily dominate the soul, becoming an addictive preoccupation. Thomas Merton commented that they are like noisy and petulant children and that indulging them only intensifies their mastery over the self. In associating messiahship with the satisfaction of personal sensual desire, the tempter is drawing Jesus away from his gathering task, for hedonism is essentially egocentric, an attempt to use the world for self-gratification.

The countermove of Jesus is to quote the Scripture: "It is written, 'One does not live by bread alone, but by every word that comes from the mouth of God'" (Matt. 4:4). How wonderful that he answers a temptation having to do with the mouth (eating) by appealing to a higher Mouth. In accord with a venerable scriptural tradition, Jesus implies that the word of God is a type of food that the human being requires even more urgently than physical nourishment, but he also orients the devil away from the inevitably self-centered quality of sensual satisfaction to the essentially communitarian quality of feasting on the divine word. God's word can be heard by all and never runs out; further, by its very nature, it is meant to be passed on once it has been taken in. It is an expression of that graced manner of being—what is had precisely as it is given away and shared—that we see in the account of the prodigal son. What Jesus tells *ho poneros* (the evil one) is that he chooses to live primarily off this food and hence to remain in the loop of grace.

The topography shifts as we move to the second temptation: "Then the devil took him to the holy city and placed him on the pinnacle of the temple" (Matt. 4:5).

We have now moved to a higher, more spiritually refined challenge. Having failed to dissuade the warrior through sensual desire, the tempter displays the allurements of the heights, what Aquinas calls *gloria*. The scatterer brings Jesus to the temple and places him at the very pinnacle of it, in a position of prominence and supreme visibility. At the tip-top of the temple, Jesus is symbolically at the very height of the society and culture of his time, master of the realms of economy, politics, and religion, the undisputed center of attention. Moreover, he even has the prospect of being the focus of the divine attention: "If you are the Son of God, throw yourself down; for it is written, 'He will command his angels concerning you,' and 'On their hands they will bear you up, so that you will not dash your foot against a stone'" (Matt. 4:6). What the devil is offering him is, in a word, the inflation of the ego through honor.

In response to Satan's temptation, Jesus once more cites the Scriptures: "Again it is written, 'Do not put the Lord your God to the test'" (Matt. 4:7). To be in the grip of the lust for honor is to need the constant attention and appreciation of the other. It is to require the other to "bear me up," inflate me, protect me from harm, no matter what I do. It is to make of another subject, even of God himself, an audience, and hence to reduce that subject to a means. In insisting that God should never be put to the test, Jesus is resisting just that spiritual danger.

For the third temptation, the scatterer raises Jesus to the loftiest possible point of vantage: "Again, the devil took him to a very high mountain and showed him all the kingdoms of the world and their splendor" (Matt. 4:8). If the lure of sensual pleasure is the most elemental temptation, and the lure of glory the intermediate, the seduction of power—the mountaintop experience—is the most sublime and dangerous. Power is obviously a positive value, since God himself is referred to as the "Almighty" one, and the mountain, the point of contact between God and the world, is in the biblical framework holy ground. The devil has thus brought Jesus into a dizzying, rarefied atmosphere, a heady place where it is not easy to distinguish the real from the apparent good. We notice here the temptation is not to be looked at (as in the last episode), but rather to look. All the kingdoms of the world are displayed from this height, and Jesus is encouraged to look out at them in a mastering way, casting his glance and his will on them simultaneously.

Having prepared his interlocutor, the tempter makes his move: "All these I will give you, if you will fall down and worship me" (Matt. 4:9). What emerges as both most illuminating and most disturbing is that the devil can offer all of the kingdoms of the world precisely because they all belong to him. This connection is made even clearer in Luke's account: "And the devil said to him, 'To you I will give their glory and all this authority; for it has been given over to me, and I give to anyone I please" (Luke 4:6). Here, the nature of the power in question becomes clear. It has nothing to do with the legitimate power by which God governs the cosmos; it has everything to do with the devil's essential task of scattering.

When Jesus resists the temptation to worship the scatterer and to become the lord of the kingdoms of the world, he is turning away from the pseudo-*ordo* that has bedeviled the human race from the beginning. "Away with you, Satan! for it is written, 'Worship the Lord your God, and serve only him'" (Matt. 4:10). Here, at the close of the ordeal, Jesus addresses the devil for the first time by name, and the choice of titles could not be more telling, for *Satan* means "the one who accuses." Jesus sends away the blamer/scapegoater in whose spirit the lords of this world exercise their authority, and he announces that the worship of God alone is the matrix for true power. At the end of his ministry, Jesus is nailed to the cross and is declared, in a supreme irony, to be the King of the Jews, the wielder of authentic authority. He hangs there accused, a scapegoat cast outside the walls of the city, but what comes from his mouth is not a curse but a prayer of forgiveness for those who are killing him. In this he shows what it means to exercise power that comes from the worship of the true God. God is the one who gives, a *communio* of grace, a fountain of forgiveness, and hence the King who worships him wields a power conditioned in every sense by love and inclusion.

# Reflection

**Fulton Sheen**

*Life of Christ*

Temptation was a negative preparation for his ministry, as baptism had been a positive preparation. In his baptism, he had received the Spirit and a confirmation of his mission; in his temptations, he received the strengthening which comes directly from trial and testing. There is a law written across the universe, that no one shall be crowned unless he has first struggled. No halo of merit rests suspended over those who do not fight. Icebergs that float in the cold streams of the north do not command our respectful attention, just for being icebergs; but if they were to float in the warm waters of the Gulf Stream without dissolving, they would command awe and wonderment. They might, if they did it on purpose, be said to have character.

The only way one can ever prove love is by making an act of choice; mere words are not enough. Hence, the original trial given to man has been given again to all men; even the angels have passed through a trial. Ice deserves no credit for being cold, nor fire for being hot; it is only those who have the possibility of choice that can be praised for their acts. It is through temptation and its strain that the depths of character are revealed. Scripture says: "Blessed is he who endures under trials. When he has proved his worth, he will win that crown of life, which God has promised to those who love him" (James 1:12).

The defenses of the soul are seen at their strongest when the evil which has been resisted is also strong. The presence of temptation does not necessarily imply moral imperfection on the part of the one who is tempted. In that case, our Divine Lord could not have been tempted at all. An inward tendency toward evil, such as man has, is not a necessary condition for an onslaught of temptation. The temptation of our Blessed Lord came only from without, and not from within as ours so often do. What was at stake in the trial of our Lord was not the perversion of natural appetites to which the rest of men are tempted; rather, it was an appeal to our Lord to disregard his Divine Mission and his Messianic work. The temptation that comes from without does not necessarily weaken character; indeed, when conquered, it affords an opportunity for holiness to increase. If he was to be the Pattern Man, he would have to teach us how to gain holiness by overcoming temptation. "It is because he himself has been tried by suffering, that he has the power to help us in the trials we undergo" (Heb. 2:18).

# Prayer

**St. John Henry Newman**
*Meditations and Devotions*

I know, O my God, I must change, if I am to see your face! I must undergo the change of death. Body and soul must die to this world. My real self, my soul, must change by a true regeneration. None but the holy can see you. Like Peter, I cannot have a blessing now, which I shall have afterwards. "You cannot follow me now, but you shall follow hereafter." Oh, support me, as I proceed in this great, awful, happy change, with the grace of your unchangeableness. My unchangeableness here below is perseverance in changing. Let me day by day be molded upon you, and be changed from glory to glory, by ever looking toward you, and ever leaning on your arm. I know, O Lord, I must go through trial, temptation, and much conflict, if I am to come to you. I know not what lies before me, but I know as much as this. I know, too, that if you are not with me, my change will be for the worse, not for the better. Whatever fortune I have, be I rich or poor, healthy or sick, with friends or without, all will turn to evil if I am not sustained by the Unchangeable; all will turn to good if I have Jesus with me, yesterday and today the same, and forever.

Amen.

# Hymn

*Lux Ecce Surgit Aurea*

## Latin

*Lux ecce surgit aurea,*
*Pallens facessat caecitas,*
*Quae nosmet in praeceps diu*
*Errore traxit devio.*

*Haec lux serenum conferat,*
*Purosque nos praestet sibi:*
*Nihil loquamur subdolum:*
*Volvamus obscurum nihil.*

*Sic tota decurrat dies,*
*Ne lingua mendax, ne manus*
*Oculive peccent lubrici,*
*Ne noxa corpus inquinet.*

*Speculator adstat desuper,*
*Qui nos diebus omnibus,*
*Actusque nostros prospicit*
*A luce prima in vesperum.*

## English

See the golden sun arise!
Let no more our darkened eyes
Snare us, tangled by surprise
In the maze of sin!

From false words and thoughts impure
Let this Light, serene and sure,
Keep our lips without secure,
Keep our souls within.

So may we the day-time spend,
That, till life's temptations end,
Tongue, nor hand, nor eye offend!
One, above us all,

Views in his revealing ray
All we do, and think, and say,
Watching us from break of day
Till the twilight fall.

*Deo Patri sit gloria,*
*Eiusque soli Filio,*
*Cum Spiritu Paraclito,*
*Nunc et per omne saeculum.*

Unto God the Father, Son,
Holy Spirit, Three in One,
One in Three, be glory done,
Now and evermore.

# Reflection

**St. Bonaventure**
*The Tree of Life*

By humbly enduring the enemy's attacks, he would make us humble; and by winning a victory, he would make us courageous. He firmly took up a life that was hard and solitary so that he might arouse the souls of the faithful to strive toward perfection and strengthen them to endure hardships.

Come now, disciple of Christ,
search into the secrets of solitude
with your loving teacher,
so that having become a companion of wild beasts,
you may become an imitator and sharer of
the hidden silence, the devout prayer, the daylong fasting,
and the three encounters with the clever enemy.
And so you will learn
to have recourse to him
in every crisis of temptation
because "we do not have a high priest
who cannot have compassion on our infirmities,
but one tried
in all things as we are,
except sin" (Heb. 4:15).

# Poem

**St. John Henry Newman**
**"Temptation"**


O Holy Lord, who with the Children Three
    Didst walk the piercing flame,
Help, in those trial-hours, which, save to Thee,
      I dare not name;
Nor let these quivering eyes and sickening heart
Crumble to dust beneath the Tempter's dart.

Thou, who didst once Thy life from Mary's breast
    Renew from day to day,
Oh, might her smile, severely sweet, but rest
      On this frail clay!
Till I am Thine with my whole soul; and fear,
Not feel a secret joy, that Hell is near.

# Prayer

**St. Thérèse of Lisieux**
**From the Prayer for Acquiring Humility**

You know my weakness, Lord. Every morning I make a resolution to practice humility and in the evening I recognize that I have committed again many faults of pride. At this I am tempted to become discouraged but I know that discouragement is also pride. Therefore, O my God, I want to base my hope in you alone. Since you can do everything, deign to bring to birth in my soul the virtue I desire. To obtain this grace of your infinite mercy I will very often repeat: "O Jesus, gentle and humble of heart, make my heart like yours!"

Amen.

"Is not the gravest temptation before which mankind marches the temptation of despair?"

—HENRI DE LUBAC

# The Fourth
# Week *of* Lent

# REPENT
# AND BELIEVE

## Scripture
**Mark 1:14–15**

After John had been arrested, Jesus came to Galilee proclaiming the gospel of God: "This is the time of fulfillment. The kingdom of God is at hand. Repent, and believe in the gospel."

## Reading
**Bishop Barron**
*And Now I See*

In Jesus' opening speech in Mark's Gospel, we hear: "Repent, and believe in the Gospel" (Mark 1:15). The word so often and so misleadingly translated as "repent" is *metanoeite*. This Greek term is based upon two words, *meta* (beyond) and *nous* (mind or spirit), and thus, in its most basic form, means something like "go beyond the mind that you have." The English word "repent" has a moralizing overtone, suggesting a change in behavior or action, whereas Jesus' term seems to be hinting at a change at a far more fundamental level of one's being. Jesus urges his listeners to change their way of knowing, their way of perceiving and grasping reality, their perspective, their mode of seeing.

What Jesus implies is this: the new state of affairs has arrived, the divine and human have met, but the way you customarily see is going to blind you to this novelty. In the Gnostic Gospel of Thomas, Jesus expresses the same concern: "The kingdom of God is spread out on the earth, *but people do not see it*." Minds, eyes, ears, senses, perceptions—all have to be opened up, turned around, revitalized. *Metanoia*, soul transformation, is Jesus' first recommendation: open your eyes; see the coming together of the divine and the human; learn to live in the power of that Incarnation (the kingdom) through *metanoia,* through the changing of your attitude, your orientation, your way of seeing.

But Jesus' great speech does not end with the call to *metanoia*; rather, it explicitly names the state of being in the kingdom of God, the goal and end point of the change of heart: "Believe in the Gospel." Now, like the word *metanoiete,* the term *pisteuete* (believe) has been terribly misunderstood over the centuries, coming, unfortunately, to mean the dry assent to religious propositions for which there is little or no evidence. Since the Enlightenment and its altogether legitimate insistence on rational responsibility, faith, in the sense just described, has come into disrepute. It seems to be the last refuge of uncritical people, those desperate to find some assurance with regard to the ultimate things and thus willing to swallow even the most far-fetched theories and beliefs.

Happily, "belief" in the biblical and traditional sense of the term has nothing to do with this truncated and irresponsible rationality. "To believe," as Jesus uses the term, signals not so much a way of knowing as a way of *being known*. To have faith is to allow oneself to be overwhelmed by the power of God, to permit the divine energy to reign at all levels of one's being. As such, it is not primarily a matter of understanding and assenting to propositions as it is surrendering to the God who wants to become incarnate in us. In Paul Tillich's language, faith is being grasped by "ultimate concern," permitting oneself to be shaken and turned by the in-breaking God.

Hence, when Jesus urges his listeners to believe, he is inviting them not so much to adhere to a new set of propositions, but rather to let go of the dominating and fearful ego and learn once more to live in the confidence of the *magna anima* (great soul). He is calling them to find the new center of their lives *where he finds his own*—namely, in the unconditional love of God. One of the tragic ironies of the tradition is that Jesus' "faith," interpreted along rationalist lines, serves only to boost up the ego, confirming it in its grasping ("I *have* the faith, and you don't") or its fear ("Do I *really* understand the statements I claim to believe?"). The state of mind designed to quell the ego has been, more often than not, transformed into one more ego game. To "believe" in the "Gospel" has nothing to do with these games of the mind. It has everything to do with a radical change of life and vision, with the simple (and dreadfully complex) process of allowing oneself to swim in the divine sea, to find the true self by letting go of the old center.

# Reflection
**Pope Benedict XVI**
**General Audience**

To repent [or convert] is to change direction in the journey of life: not, however, by means of a small adjustment, but with a true and proper about turn. Conversion means swimming against the tide, where the "tide" is the superficial lifestyle, inconsistent and deceptive, that often sweeps us along, overwhelms us, and makes us slaves to evil or at any rate prisoners of moral mediocrity. With conversion, on the other hand, we are aiming for the high standard of Christian living; we entrust ourselves to the living and personal Gospel which is Jesus Christ. He is our final goal and the profound meaning of conversion, he is the path on which all are called to walk through life, letting themselves be illumined by his light and sustained by his power which moves our steps. In this way conversion expresses his most splendid and fascinating Face: it is not a mere moral decision that rectifies our conduct in life, but rather a choice of faith that wholly involves us in close communion with Jesus as a real and living Person. To repent and believe in the Gospel are not two different things or in some way only juxtaposed, but express the same reality. Repentance is the total "yes" of those who consign their whole life to the Gospel, responding freely to Christ who first offers himself to humankind as the Way, the Truth, and the Life, as the only One who sets us free and saves us. This is the precise meaning of the first words with which, according to the Evangelist Mark, Jesus begins preaching the "Gospel of God": "The time is fulfilled, and the Kingdom of God is at hand; repent, and believe in the Gospel" (Mark 1:15).

The "Repent, and believe in the Gospel" is not only at the beginning of Christian life but accompanies it throughout, endures, is renewed and spreads, branching out into all its expressions. Every day is a favorable moment of grace because every day presses us to give ourselves to Jesus, to trust in him, to abide in him, to share his lifestyle, to learn true love from him, to follow him in the daily fulfilment of the Father's will, the one great law of life. Every day, even when it is fraught with difficulties and toil, weariness and setbacks, even when we are tempted to leave the path of the following of Christ and withdraw into ourselves, into our selfishness, without realizing our need to open ourselves to the love of God in Christ, to live the same logic of justice and love.

# Prayer

**St. Teresa of Avila**

*Soliloquies*

O Lord, my God, how you possess the words of eternal life, where all mortals will find what they desire if they want to seek it! But what a strange thing, my God, that we forget your words in the madness and sickness our evil deeds cause! . . .

Oh, what great blindness, that we seek rest where it is impossible to find it! Have mercy, Creator, on these your creatures. Behold, we don't understand or know what we desire, nor do we obtain what we ask for. Lord, give us light; behold, the need is greater than with the man born blind, for he wanted to see the light and couldn't. Now, Lord, there is no desire to see. Oh, how incurable an illness! Here, my God, is where your power must be demonstrated; here, your mercy.

Oh, what a difficult thing I ask you, my true God: that you love someone who doesn't love you, that you open to one who doesn't knock, that you give health to one who likes to be sick and goes about looking for sickness. You say, my Lord, that you come to seek sinners; these, Lord, are real sinners. Don't look at our blindness, my God, but at all the blood your Son shed for us. Let your mercy shine upon evil that has so increased; behold, Lord, we are your handiwork. May your goodness and mercy help us.

Amen.

# Hymn

*Attende Domine*

## Latin

*Attende Domine, et miserere,*
*quia peccavimus tibi.*

*Ad te Rex summe,*
*omnium redemptor,*
*Oculos nostros*
*sublevamus flentes:*
*Exaudi, Christe,*
*supplicantum preces.*
(REFRAIN)

*Dextera Patris,*
*lapis angularis,*
*Via salutis,*
*ianua caelestis,*
*Ablue nostri*
*maculas delicti.*
(REFRAIN)

## English

Hear us, O Lord, and have mercy,
because we have sinned against thee.

To thee, highest King,
Redeemer of all,
do we lift up our eyes
in weeping:
Hear, O Christ, the prayers
of your servants.
(REFRAIN)

Right hand of the Father,
corner-stone,
way of salvation,
gate of heaven,
wash away our
stains of sin.
(REFRAIN)

*Rogamus, Deus,*
*tuam majestatem:*
*Auribus sacris*
*gemitus exaudi:*
*Crimina nostra*
*placidus indulge.*
(REFRAIN)

*Tibi fatemur*
*crimina admissa:*
*Contrito corde*
*pandimus occulta:*
*Tua, Redemptor,*
*pietas ignoscat.*
(REFRAIN)

*Innocens captus,*
*nec repugnans ductus,*
*Testibus falsis,*
*pro impiis damnatus:*
*Quos redemisti,*
*tu conserva, Christe.*
(REFRAIN)

We beseech thee, God,
in thy great majesty:
Hear our groans
with thy holy ears:
calmly forgive
our crimes.
(REFRAIN)

To thee we confess
our sins admitted
with a contrite heart
We reveal the things hidden:
by thy kindness, O Redeemer,
overlook them.
(REFRAIN)

The Innocent, seized,
not refusing to be led;
condemned by false witnesses
because of impious men:
O Christ, keep safe those
whom thou hast redeemed.
(REFRAIN)

91

# Reflection

**St. Benedict**
*The Rule*

See how the Lord in his love shows us the way of life. Clothed then with faith and the performance of good works, let us set out on this way, with the Gospel for our guide, that we may deserve to see him "who has called us to his kingdom" (1 Thess. 2:12). . . .

The Lord waits for us daily to translate into action, as we should, his holy teachings. Therefore our life span has been lengthened by way of a truce, that we may amend our misdeeds. As the Apostle says: "Do you not know that the patience of God is leading you to repent?" (Rom. 2:4). And indeed the Lord assures us in his love: "I do not wish the death of the sinner, but that he turn back to me and live" (Ezek. 33:11). . . .

Do not be daunted immediately by fear and run away from the road that leads to salvation. It is bound to be narrow at the outset. But as we progress in this way of life and in faith, we shall run on the path of God's commandments, our hearts overflowing with the inexpressible delight of love.

# Poem

**G.K. Chesterton**
**"The Convert"**

After one moment when I bowed my head
And the whole world turned over and came upright,
And I came out where the old road shone white.
I walked the ways and heard what all men said,
Forests of tongues, like autumn leaves unshed,
Being not unlovable but strange and light;
Old riddles and new creeds, not in despite
But softly, as men smile about the dead.

The sages have a hundred maps to give
That trace their crawling cosmos like a tree,
They rattle reason out through many a sieve
That stores the sand and lets the gold go free:
And all these things are less than dust to me
Because my name is Lazarus and I live.

# Prayer

**St. Thérèse of Lisieux**
**Prayer to Jesus in the Tabernacle**

O God hidden in the prison of the tabernacle! I come with joy to you each evening to thank you for the graces you have given me. I ask pardon for the faults I committed today, which has just slipped away like a dream. . . .

O Jesus! how happy I would be if I had been faithful, but alas! often in the evening I am sad because I feel I could have corresponded better with your graces. . . . If I were more united to you, more charitable . . . more humble and more mortified, I would feel less sorrow when I talk with you in prayer. And yet, O my God, very far from becoming discouraged at the sight of my miseries, I come to you with confidence, recalling that "those who are well do not need a doctor but the sick do" (Luke 5:31). I beg you, then, to cure me and to pardon me. I will keep in mind, Lord, "that the soul to whom you have forgiven more should also love you more than the others"! . . . I offer you every beat of my heart as so many acts of love and reparation and I unite them to your infinite merits. I beg you, O my Divine Bridegroom, to be the Restorer of my soul, to act in me despite my resistance; and lastly, I wish to have no other will but yours. . . .

Thus, after coming each evening to the foot of your Altar, I will finally reach the last evening of my life. Then will begin for me the unending day of eternity when I will place in your Divine Heart the struggles of exile!

Amen.

"The conversion demanded of us is in no way a backward step, as sin is. It is rather a setting out, an advancement in true freedom and in joy."

—POPE ST. PAUL VI

# The Fifth
# Week *of* Lent


# THE SUFFERING
# SERVANT

# Scripture
**Isaiah 52:13–53:12**

See, my servant shall prosper,
> he shall be raised high and greatly exalted.
Even as many were amazed at him—
> so marred was his look beyond human semblance
> and his appearance beyond that of the sons of man—
so shall he startle many nations,
> because of him kings shall stand speechless;
for those who have not been told shall see,
> those who have not heard shall ponder it.


Who would believe what we have heard?
> To whom has the arm of the LORD been revealed?
He grew up like a sapling before him,
> like a shoot from the parched earth;
there was in him no stately bearing to make us look at him,
> nor appearance that would attract us to him.
He was spurned and avoided by people,
> a man of suffering, accustomed to infirmity,
one of those from whom people hide their faces,
> spurned, and we held him in no esteem.


Yet it was our infirmities that he bore,
> our sufferings that he endured,

while we thought of him as stricken,
    as one smitten by God and afflicted.
But he was pierced for our offenses,
    crushed for our sins;
upon him was the chastisement that makes us whole,
    by his stripes we were healed.
We had all gone astray like sheep,
    each following his own way;
but the LORD laid upon him
    the guilt of us all.

Though he was harshly treated, he submitted
    and opened not his mouth;
like a lamb led to the slaughter
    or a sheep before the shearers,
    he was silent and opened not his mouth.
Oppressed and condemned, he was taken away,
    and who would have thought any more of his destiny?
When he was cut off from the land of the living,
    and smitten for the sin of his people,
a grave was assigned him among the wicked
    and a burial place with evildoers,
though he had done no wrong
    nor spoken any falsehood.
But the LORD was pleased
    to crush him in infirmity.

If he gives his life as an offering for sin,
>>he shall see his descendants in a long life,
>>and the will of the LORD shall be accomplished through
>>>him.

Because of his affliction
>>he shall see the light in fullness of days;
through his suffering, my servant shall justify many,
>>and their guilt he shall bear.
Therefore I will give him his portion among the great,
>>and he shall divide the spoils with the mighty,
because he surrendered himself to death
>>and was counted among the wicked;
and he shall take away the sins of many,
>>and win pardon for their offenses.

## Reading

**Bishop Barron**
*Light from Light*

When someone presented himself at the Jerusalem temple to make a sacrifice, he would bring an unblemished animal—bull, sheep, goat, or dove—and would, with the assistance of the priest, slit the animal's throat while the priest caught the blood in a bowl. Then the beast would be burned, either whole (a holocaust) or partially, returning it thereby to God. The spiritual psychology behind the gesture seems to have been this: what is happening to this animal should, by rights, be happening to me. The goat or bull was, as it were, standing in for the person who offered it, representing him in a quasi-sacramental manner.

This substitutionary dynamic was on particularly clear display on the Day of Atonement, the one day in the Jewish liturgical year when the high priest was allowed to enter the Holy of Holies in the temple. He slaughtered and sacrificed a number of animals in the course of the day, but the spiritual highpoint was the symbolic imposition of the sins of Israel onto the scapegoat within the Holy of Holies. The animal so burdened was then driven from the temple and, led by a priest, brought deep into the desert where he was abandoned to certain death. Symbolically, he thereby bore away the sins of the people, representing both their degradation and their repentance before God. Again, though unfamiliar to us, this sort of representational thinking was absolutely standard within the cultural framework of the biblical authors. The idea perdured to the dawn of modern times in the figure of the monarch, who, in a very real way, represented all the people; we can also see it in the story of David and Goliath, in which two individuals fought in the name of their respective armies.

There was, even within the Old Testament, furthermore, an analogy between the animal sacrifice offered in the temple and a sin-offering sacrifice made directly by a human being, representative of the entire nation. I am referring, of course, to a series of mysterious and extraordinary texts in the fifty-second and fifty-third chapters of the book of the prophet Isaiah. The prophet envisions a time when the God of Israel would be victorious, but then he segues almost immediately into the surprising description of the one through whom that victory would be won: "See, my servant shall prosper; he shall be exalted and lifted up, and shall be very high. Just as there were many who were astonished at him—so marred was his appearance, beyond human semblance, and his form beyond that of mortals—so he shall startle many nations" (Isa. 52:13–15).

But why is his appearance so repellant? "He was despised and rejected by others; a man of suffering and acquainted with infirmity. . . . Surely he has borne our infirmities and carried our diseases. . . . He was wounded for our transgressions, crushed for our iniquities; upon him was the punishment that made us whole, and by his bruises we are healed" (Isa. 53:4–5). His degradation, in a word, was the direct result of his functioning as the lamb of sacrifice and the scapegoat for the entire people. What would happen to him should by rights be happening to the whole of Israel; the sins of the entire nation would be placed upon his shoulders so that he could bear them away. Though, as we have said, this kind of representational thinking is rather foreign to our individualistic social psychology, it was altogether standard for ancient Israel.

Just as the animals brought to the temple for sacrifice should be unblemished, so this suffering servant would be a man of righteousness and innocence: "He was oppressed, and he was afflicted, yet he did not open his mouth; like a lamb that is led to the slaughter, and like a sheep that before its shearers is silent, so he did not open his mouth" (Isa. 53:7). After his death, they would bury him with the wicked, "although he had done no violence, and there was no deceit in his mouth" (Isa. 53:9). His complete moral integrity would appear to be a condition for the possibility of his performing his sacrificial function, since otherwise he would presumably have to make reparation for his own sins. To bear the sins of the whole nation, he would have to be sinless: "The righteous one, my servant, shall make many righteous" (Isa. 53:11). In light of temple practice and these extraordinary texts, it is not difficult to see why the first Christians reached for sacrificial language when attempting to explain the significance of Jesus' terrible death. They saw an innocent man, their sinless Lord, indeed someone who, even in the midst of the agony of crucifixion, uttered not a curse but a blessing on those who were killing him, taking upon himself a thoroughly undeserved punishment. Like the lamb of sacrifice, they thought, his blood was being poured out as a substitute for our blood; like the scapegoat, he was being driven into the wilderness to die, as by rights we should.

# Reflection
*Catechism of the Catholic Church*
**601**

The Scriptures had foretold this divine plan of salvation through the putting to death of "the righteous one, my Servant" as a mystery of universal redemption, that is, as the ransom that would free men from the slavery of sin (Isa. 53:11; see Isa. 53:12; John 8:34–36; Acts 3:14). Citing a confession of faith that he himself had "received," St. Paul professes that "Christ died for our sins in accordance with the scriptures" (1 Cor. 15:3; see also Acts 3:18; 7:52; 13:29; 26:22–23). In particular Jesus' redemptive death fulfills Isaiah's prophecy of the suffering Servant (see Isa. 53:7–8 and Acts 8:32–35). Indeed Jesus himself explained the meaning of his life and death in the light of God's suffering Servant (see Matt. 20:28). After his Resurrection he gave this interpretation of the Scriptures to the disciples at Emmaus, and then to the apostles (see Luke 24:25–27, 44–45).

# Prayer

**Thomas à Kempis**
*The Imitation of Christ*

O Lord, I shall suffer willingly for your sake whatever you wish to send me. I am ready to accept from your hand both good and evil alike, the sweet and the bitter together, sorrow with joy; and for all that happens to me I am grateful. Keep me from all sin and I will fear neither death nor hell. Do not cast me out forever nor blot me out of the Book of Life, and whatever tribulation befalls will not harm me.

Amen.

# Hymn

*O Deus, Ego Amo Te*

**Latin**

*O Deus, ego amo te,*
*Nec amo te, ut salves me,*
*Aut quia non amantes te*
*Aeterno punis igne.*

*Tu, tu, mi Iesu, totum me*
*Amplexus es in cruce;*
*Tulisti clavos, lanceam,*
*Multamque ignominiam,*

*Innumeros dolores,*
*Sudores, et angores,*
*Et mortem, et haec propter me,*
*Ac pro me peccatore.*

*Cur igitur non amem te,*
*O Iesu amantissime,*
*Non, ut in coelo salves me,*
*Aut ne aeternum damnes me,*

## English

My God, I love thee, not because
I hope for heaven thereby;
Nor yet since they who love thee not
Must burn eternally.

Thou, O my Jesus, thou didst me
Upon the cross embrace;
For me didst bear the nails and spear,
And manifold disgrace;

And griefs and torments numberless,
And sweat of agony;
E'en death itself; and all for one
Who was thine enemy.

Then why, O blessed Jesus Christ,
Should I not love thee well,
Not for the sake of winning heaven,
Or of escaping hell;

*Nec praemii ullius spe,*
*Sed sicut tu amasti me?*
*Sic amo et amabo te,*


*Solum quia Rex meus es,*
*Et solum quia Deus es.*

Not with the hope of gaining aught,
Not seeking a reward;
But as thyself hast loved me,
O ever-loving Lord?

E'en so I love thee, and will love,
And in thy praise will sing,
Solely because thou art my God,
And my eternal King.

# Reflection

**Pope St. John Paul II**
*Salvifici Doloris*

The Scriptures had to be fulfilled. There were many messianic texts in the Old Testament which foreshadowed the sufferings of the future Anointed One of God. Among all these, particularly touching is the one which is commonly called the *Fourth Song of the Suffering Servant*, in the Book of Isaiah. The Prophet, who has rightly been called "the Fifth Evangelist," presents in this Song an image of the sufferings of the Servant with a realism as acute as if he were seeing them with his own eyes: the eyes of the body and of the spirit. In the light of the verses of Isaiah, the Passion of Christ becomes almost more expressive and touching than in the descriptions of the Evangelists themselves. Behold, the true Man of Sorrows presents himself before us. . . .

The Song of the Suffering Servant contains a description in which it is possible, in a certain sense, to identify the stages of Christ's Passion in their various details: the arrest, the humiliation, the blows, the spitting, the contempt for the prisoner, the unjust sentence, and then the scourging, the crowning with thorns and the mocking, the carrying of the cross, the Crucifixion and the agony.

Even more than this description of the Passion, what strikes us in the words of the Prophet *is the depth of Christ's sacrifice*. Behold, he, though innocent, takes upon himself the sufferings of all people, because he takes upon himself the sins of all. "The Lord has laid on him the iniquity of us all": *all* human sin in its breadth and depth becomes the true cause of the Redeemer's suffering. If the suffering "is measured" by the evil suffered, then the words of the Prophet enable us to understand *the extent of this evil* and suffering with which Christ burdened himself. It can be said that this is "substitutive" suffering; but above all it is "redemptive." The Man of Sorrows of that prophecy is truly that "Lamb of God who takes away the sin of the world" (John 1:29). In his suffering, sins are canceled out precisely because he alone as the only-begotten Son could take them upon himself, accept them *with that love for the Father which overcomes* the evil of every sin; in a certain sense he annihilates this evil in the spiritual space of the relationship between God and humanity, and fills this space with good.

# Poem

**St. Teresa of Avila**

**"For the Profession of Isabel de Los Angeles"**

In weeping be my joy,
My rest in fright,
In sorrowing my serenity,
My wealth in losing all.

Amid storms be my love,
In the wound my delight.
My life in death,
In rejection my favor.

In poverty be my riches,
My triumph in struggling,
Rest in laboring,
In sadness my contentment.

In darkness be my light,
My greatness in the lowly place,
My way on the short road,
In the cross my glory.

In humiliation be my honor,
My palm in suffering
Increase in my wanting
In losing my gain.

My fullness be in hunger,
In fearing my hope,
My rejoicing in fear,
In grieving my delight.

In forgetting be my memory,
Humiliation my exalting,
In lowliness my repute,
Affronts my victory.

My laurels be in contempt,
In afflictions my fondness,
My dignity a lowly nook,
In solitude my esteem.

In Christ be my trust,
My affection in him alone,
In his weariness my vigor,
My repose in his imitation.

My strength is founded here,
In him alone is my surety,
My integrity's proof,
In his likeness my purity.

# Prayer

**St. Thérèse of Lisieux**

*Story of a Soul*

"You have given me *delight*, O Lord, in *all* your doings." For is there a *joy* greater than that of suffering out of love for you? The more interior the suffering is and the less apparent to the eyes of creatures, the more it rejoices you, O my God! But if my suffering was really unknown to you, which is impossible, I would still be happy to have it, if through it I could prevent or make reparation for one single sin against faith.

Amen.

"Jesus identifies himself
with all victims."

—RENÉ GIRARD

Palm Sunday

# THE ENTRY INTO JERUSALEM

# Scripture
**John 12:12–19**

When the great crowd that had come to the feast heard that Jesus was coming to Jerusalem, they took palm branches and went out to meet him, and cried out,

> "Hosanna!
> Blessed is he who comes in the name of the Lord,
> the king of Israel."

Jesus found an ass and sat upon it, as is written:

> *Fear no more, O daughter Zion;*
> *see, your king comes, seated upon an ass's colt.*

His disciples did not understand this at first, but when Jesus had been glorified they remembered that these things were written about him and that they had done this for him. So the crowd that was with him when he called Lazarus from the tomb and raised him from death continued to testify. This was also why the crowd went to meet him, because they heard that he had done this sign. So the Pharisees said to one another, "You see that you are gaining nothing. Look, the whole world has gone after him."

# Reading

**Bishop Barron**

*Vibrant Paradoxes*

The texts that Christians typically read on Palm Sunday have become so familiar that most probably don't sense their properly revolutionary power. But no first-century Jew would have missed the excitement and danger implicit in the coded language of the accounts describing Jesus' entry into Jerusalem just a few days before his death.

In Mark's Gospel, we hear that Jesus and his disciples "were approaching Jerusalem, at Bethphage and Bethany, near the Mount of Olives" (Mark 11:1). A bit of trivial geographical detail, we might be tempted to conclude. But we have to remember that pious Jews of Jesus' time were immersed in the infinitely complex world of the Hebrew Scriptures and stubbornly read everything through the lens provided by those writings.

About five hundred years before Jesus' time, the prophet Ezekiel had relayed a vision of the *Shekinah* (the glory) of Yahweh leaving the temple due to its corruption: "The glory of the LORD went out from the threshold of the house [the temple] and stopped above the cherubim. The cherubim . . . rose up from the earth in my sight as they went out. . . . They stopped at the entrance of the east gate of the house of the LORD; and the glory of the God of Israel was above them"

(Ezek. 10:18–19). This was one of the most devastating texts in the Old Testament. The temple of the Lord was seen as, in almost a literal sense, the dwelling place of God, the meeting place of heaven and earth. Thus, even to imagine that the glory of the Lord had quit his temple was shocking in the extreme. However, Ezekiel also prophesied that one day the glory of God would return to the temple, and precisely from the same direction in which it had left: "Then he brought me to the gate, the gate facing east. And there, the glory of the God of Israel was coming from the east; the sound was like the sound of mighty waters; and the earth shone with his glory" (Ezek. 43:1–2). Furthermore, upon the return of the Lord's glory, Ezekiel predicted, the corrupt temple would be cleansed, restored, rebuilt.

Now let's return to Jesus, who, during his public ministry, consistently spoke and acted in the very person of God and who said, in reference to himself, "Something greater than the temple is here" (Matt. 12:6). As the Jews of Jesus' day saw him approaching Jerusalem from the east, they would have remembered Ezekiel's vision and would have begun to entertain the wild but thrilling idea that perhaps this Jesus was, in person, the glory of Yahweh returning to his dwelling place on earth. And, in light of this, they would have understood the bewildering acts that Jesus performed in the temple. He was, in fact, another Ezekiel, pronouncing judgment on the old temple and then announcing a magnificent rebuilding campaign: "Destroy this temple, and in three days I will raise it up" (John 2:19). Jesus, they came to understand, was the new and definitive temple, the meeting place of heaven and earth.

And there is even more to see in the drama of Jesus' arrival in the holy city. As the rabbi from Nazareth entered Jerusalem on a donkey, no one could have missed the reference to a passage in the book of the prophet Zechariah: "Rejoice greatly, O daughter Zion! Shout aloud, O daughter Jerusalem! Lo, your king comes to you; triumphant and victorious is he, humble and riding on a donkey, on a colt, the foal of a donkey" (Zech. 9:9). A thousand years before the time of Jesus, David had taken possession of Jerusalem, dancing before the ark of the covenant. David's son Solomon built the great temple in David's city in order to house the ark, and therefore, for that brief, shining moment, Israel was ruled by righteous kings. But then Solomon himself and a whole slew of his descendants fell into corruption, and the prophets felt obligated to criticize the kings as thoroughly as they criticized the temple. The people began to long for the return of the king, for the appearance of the true David, the one who would deal with the enemies of the nation and rule as king of the world. They expected this new David, of course, to be a human figure, but something else rather surprising colored their expectation—namely, that through this human being, God would personally come to rule the

121

nation. Here are just two passages, chosen from dozens, that express this hope: "For I am a great King, says the Lord of hosts, and my name is reverenced among the nations" (Mal. 1:14); and "I will extol you, my God and King, and bless your name forever. . . . Your kingdom is an everlasting kingdom, and your dominion endures throughout all generations" (Ps. 145:1, 13). So, to draw these various strands together, we might say that the biblical authors expected Yahweh to become king, precisely through a son of David, who would enter the holy city not as a conquering hero, riding a stately Arabian charger, but as a humble figure, riding a young donkey. Could anyone have missed that this was exactly what they were seeing on Palm Sunday? Jesus was not only the glory of Yahweh returning to his temple; he was also the new David, indeed Yahweh himself, reclaiming his city and preparing to deal with the enemies of Israel.

He fought, of course, not in the conventional manner. Instead, he took all of the dysfunction of the world upon himself and swallowed it up in the ocean of the divine mercy and forgiveness. He thereby dealt with the enemies of the nation and emerged as the properly constituted king of the world. And this is why Pontius Pilate, placing over the cross a sign in Latin, Greek, and Hebrew announcing that this crucified Jesus is King of the Jews, became, despite himself, the first great evangelist!

And so the message, delivered in the wonderfully coded and ironic language of the Gospel writers, still resonates today: heaven and earth have come together; God is victorious; Jesus is Lord.

# Reflection

*Catechism of the Catholic Church*
**559–560**

How will Jerusalem welcome her Messiah? Although Jesus had always refused popular attempts to make him king, he chooses the time and prepares the details for his messianic entry into the city of "his father David" (Luke 1:32; see Matt. 21:1–11; John 6:15). Acclaimed as son of David, as the one who brings salvation (*Hosanna* means "Save!" or "Give salvation!"), the "King of glory" enters his City "riding on an ass" (Ps. 24:7–10; Zech. 9:9). Jesus conquers the Daughter of Zion, a figure of his Church, neither by ruse nor by violence, but by the humility that bears witness to the truth (see John 18:37). And so the subjects of his kingdom on that day are children and God's poor, who acclaim him as had the angels when they announced him to the shepherds (see Matt. 21:15–16; see Ps. 8:3; Luke 19:38; 2:14). Their acclamation, "Blessed be he who comes in the name of the Lord" (see Ps. 118:26) is taken up by the Church in the "*Sanctus*" of the Eucharistic liturgy that introduces the memorial of the Lord's Passover.

*Jesus' entry into Jerusalem* manifested the coming of the kingdom that the King-Messiah was going to accomplish by the Passover of his Death and Resurrection. It is with the celebration of that entry on Palm Sunday that the Church's liturgy solemnly opens Holy Week.

124

# Prayer
## The Didache
## Chapter 10

We thank you, holy Father, for your holy name which you have caused to dwell in our hearts, and for the knowledge and faith and immortality, which you have made known to us through Jesus your Son; to you be glory forever. You, Lord Almighty, have created all things for your name's sake (Wis. 1:14; Sir. 18:1; 24:8; Rev. 4:11; Isa. 43:7) and have given food and drink to men for their refreshment, so that they might render thanks to you; but upon us you have bestowed spiritual food and drink, and life everlasting through your Son (John 6:27). For all things we render you thanks, because you are mighty; to you be glory forever. Remember, O Lord, your Church, deliver it from all evil (Matt. 6:13; John 17:15) and make it perfect in your love and gather it from the four winds (Matt. 24:31), sanctified for your kingdom, which you have prepared for it; for yours is the power and the glory forever. Let grace come, and let this world pass away, "Hosanna to the God of David" (Matt. 21:9, 15). If anyone is Holy, let him come; if anyone is not, let him repent. *Maranatha* (1 Cor. 16:22; see Rev. 22:20). Amen.

# Hymn

*Gloria, Laus, et Honor*

## Latin

REFRAIN:
*Gloria, laus, et honor,*
*tibi sit Rex Christe Redemptor:*
*Cui puerile decus prompsit*
*Hosanna pium.*

*Israel es tu Rex, Davidis et*
*inclyta proles:*
*Nomine qui in Domini,*
*Rex benedicte, venis.*
(REFRAIN)

*Coetus in excelsis te laudat*
*coelicus omnis,*
*Et mortalis homo, et cuncta*
*creata simul.*
(REFRAIN)

## English

All glory, laud, and honor
To thee, Redeemer, King,
To whom the lips of children
Made sweet hosannas ring.

Thou art the King of Israel,
Thou David's royal Son,
Who in the Lord's Name comest,
The King and Blessed One.
(REFRAIN)

The company of angels
Are praising thee on high,
And mortal men and all things
Created·make reply.
(REFRAIN)

*Plebs Hebraea tibi cum palmis*
*obvia venit:*
*Cum prece, voto, hymnis,*
*adsumus ecce tibi.*
(REFRAIN)

*Et tibi passuro solvebant*
*munia laudis:*
*Nos tibi regnanti pangimus*
*ecce melos.*
(REFRAIN)

*Hi placuere tibi, placeat*
*devotio nostra:*
*Rex bone, Rex clemens, cui*
*bona cuncta placent.*
(REFRAIN)

The people of the Hebrews
With palms before thee went;
Our praise and prayer and anthems
Before thee we present.
(REFRAIN)

To thee before thy Passion
They sang their hymns of praise;
To thee now high exalted
Our melody we raise.
(REFRAIN)

Thou didst accept their praises,
Accept the prayers we bring,
Who in all good delightest,
Thou good and gracious King.
(REFRAIN)

# Reflection

**St. Irenaeus**

*Against Heresies*

The one and the same Lord [has] granted, by means of his advent, a greater gift of grace to those of a later period, than what he had granted to those under the Old Testament dispensation. For they indeed used to hear, by means of [his] servants, that the King would come, and they rejoiced to a certain extent, inasmuch as they hoped for his coming; but those who have beheld him actually present, and have obtained liberty, and been made partakers of his gifts, do possess a greater amount of grace, and a higher degree of exultation, rejoicing because of the King's arrival: as also David says, "My soul shall rejoice in the Lord; it shall be glad in his salvation" (Ps. 35:9).

And for this cause, upon his entrance into Jerusalem, all those who were in the way [of David] recognized David their king in his sorrow of soul, and spread their garments for him, and ornamented the way with green boughs, crying out with great joy and gladness, "Hosanna to the Son of David; blessed is he that comes in the name of the Lord: hosanna in the highest" (Matt. 21:9). But to the envious wicked stewards, who circumvented those under them, and ruled over those that had no great intelligence, and for this reason were unwilling that the king should come, and who said to him,

"Do you hear what these say?" did the Lord reply, "Have you never read, 'Out of the mouths of babes and sucklings have you perfected praise'?" (Matt. 21:16)—thus pointing out that what had been declared by David concerning the Son of God, was accomplished in his own person; and indicating that they were indeed ignorant of the meaning of the Scripture and the dispensation of God; but declaring that it was himself who was announced by the prophets as Christ, whose name is praised in all the earth, and who perfects praise to his Father from the mouth of babes and sucklings; wherefore also his glory has been raised above the heavens.

# Poem

**G.K. Chesterton**
**"The Donkey"**

When fishes flew and forests walked
    And figs grew upon thorn,
Some moment when the moon was blood
    Then surely I was born.

With monstrous head and sickening cry
    And ears like errant wings,
The devil's walking parody
    On all four-footed things.

The tattered outlaw of the earth,
    Of ancient crooked will;
Starve, scourge, deride me: I am dumb,
    I keep my secret still.

Fools! For I also had my hour;
    One far fierce hour and sweet:
There was a shout about my ears,
    And palms before my feet.

# Prayer

**St. Thérèse of Lisieux**
**From "He Who Has Jesus Has Everything"**

Jesus, you are the Lamb I love.
You are all I need, O supreme good!
In you I have everything, the earth and even Heaven.
The Flower that I pick, O my King,
Is You!
Amen.

"He had often entered Jerusalem before, but never with so much circumstance…. When he had both given them sufficient proof of his power, and the cross was at the doors, he makes himself then more conspicuous, and does with greater circumstance all the things that were likely to inflame them."

—ST. JOHN CHRYSOSTOM

Monday *of*
Holy Week


# THE CLEANSING
# OF THE TEMPLE

# Scripture
**Matthew 21:12–17**

Jesus entered the temple area and drove out all those engaged in selling and buying there. He overturned the tables of the money changers and the seats of those who were selling doves. And he said to them, "It is written:

'My house shall be a house of prayer,'

but you are making it a den of thieves."

The blind and the lame approached him in the temple area, and he cured them. When the chief priests and the scribes saw the wondrous things he was doing, and the children crying out in the temple area, "Hosanna to the Son of David," they were indignant and said to him, "Do you hear what they are saying?" Jesus said to them, "Yes; and have you never read the text,

'Out of the mouths of infants and nurslings

you have brought forth praise'?"

And leaving them, he went out of the city to Bethany, and there he spent the night.

# Reading

**Bishop Barron**

*Vibrant Paradoxes*

Artistic representations of the Ten Commandments often depict two stone tablets on which there are two tables of inscriptions. This portrayal follows from a classical division of the commandments in which there are two specific categories—those that order humanity's relationship with God and those that order human relationships with one another. If we consider the Bible as a totality, it becomes apparent that the Scriptures give priority to the first table, those commands dealing with God.

The Ten Commandments begin with an insistence that the Lord alone is God and there are to be no other gods besides him. This is not just a principle meant to order humanity's expressions of ritualized worship but a statement about the ethos of the entire moral and spiritual order. Whatever it is that humanity worships, be it the gods of the ancients or the allures of wealth, power, pleasure, and honor, will by necessity give rise to our perceptions and practices concerning the moral life. The God or gods in whom we place our ultimate concern will direct our lives and determine our choices.

Given that the Bible calls humanity over and over again to relinquish its attachment to false gods and embrace the worship of the one true God, we might take that emphasis as a means to interpret Christ's actions in regard to the money changers in the Jerusalem temple, actions that are traditionally referred to as the "cleansing of the temple." The dramatic scene portrays Christ entering the sacred center of Israel's culture and worship at the height of the Jewish year—the feast of Passover. Christ then raises a ruckus, for he finds the temple to be not a house of prayer but a "marketplace." He turns over the tables of the moneychangers, disrupts the trade in animals for sacrifice, and cleans the place out.

This scene is often interpreted as testimony against materialism in religious practice. Religion is to remain radically pure in regard to the corruptions of commerce. An idealism emerges from this interpretation that engenders a hair-trigger with respect to any and all associations of religion with economics or money. According to this conceit, the only way forward for religion is to maintain its purity by eschewing the corrupting influence of commerce.

While sharing the aversion to using religion as a means to gain material wealth, I think a more fruitful way of understanding Christ's action to cleanse the temple can be discerned in relation to Israel's aversion to the worship of false gods and the necessity of cleansing our own temple— that is, our lives—of these fallen deities. Remember, St.

Paul said that the body of each Christian is "a temple of the Holy Spirit" (1 Cor. 6:19). By this, he means a place where the one true God is honored and worshiped. The Apostle is providing us with an image of the Christian life as one in which a person finds happiness and integration in the measure that she becomes, personally, a place where God is first.

Think, then, that Christ has come not only to "cleanse the temple of Jerusalem" but the temple of your own body, your own life. The Lord Jesus comes into your life expecting to find a place ordered to the worship of the one true God, but what he finds is "a marketplace." What does this mean? It means that Christ finds a place where things other than God have become primary. To bring such idolatry closer to our cultural experience, how much of your life is given over to materialism, commercialism, or the accumulation of things? What rivals to the one true God have you allowed to invade the sacred space of your soul? Earlier, I referenced wealth, pleasure, power, and honor. How are these things enshrined in the sanctuary of your own heart?

The temple-cleansing Christ is a memorable image with enduring power. We shouldn't relegate that image or the Lord himself to merely a statement about our impatience with the corruptions of religious institutions and miss the point that strikes closer to home: Christ comes to each of us to rid the temple of our own body of the idols to which we have foolishly given power and pride of place.

# Reflection

**Pope Benedict XVI**
*Jesus of Nazareth: Part Two: Holy Week*

In Mark's Gospel, the false witness accuses Jesus of saying: "I will destroy this temple that is made with hands, and in three days I will build another, not made with hands" (Mark 14:58). The "witness" probably comes quite close to Jesus' actual words, but he is mistaken in one crucial point: it is not Jesus who destroys the temple—it is those who turn it into a den of robbers who abandon it to destruction, just as in Jeremiah's day [see Jer. 7:11].

In John's Gospel, Jesus' actual words are rendered thus: "Destroy this temple, and in three days I will raise it up" (John 2:19). This was how Jesus responded to the Jewish officials' demand for a sign to demonstrate his authority for acting as he did in the cleansing of the temple. His "sign" is the cross and Resurrection. The cross and Resurrection give him authority as the one who ushers in true worship. Jesus justifies himself through his Passion—the sign of Jonah that he gives to Israel and to the world.

Yet this saying has an even deeper significance. As John rightly says, the disciples understood it in its full depth only after the Resurrection, in their memory—in the collective memory of the community of disciples enlightened by the Holy Spirit, that is, the Church.

The rejection and Crucifixion of Jesus means at the same time the end of this temple. The era of the temple is over. A new worship is being introduced, in a Temple not built by human hands. This Temple is his body, the Risen One, who gathers the peoples and unites them in the sacrament of his Body and Blood. He himself is the new Temple of humanity. The Crucifixion of Jesus is at the same time the destruction of the old temple. With his Resurrection, a new way of worshiping God begins, no longer on this or that mountain, but "in spirit and truth" (John 4:23). . . .

At the time of the cleansing of the temple, the disciples remembered that it is written: "Zeal for your house will consume me" (John 2:17). This is taken from the great "Passion Psalm" 69. Living according to God's word leads to the Psalmist's isolation; for him it becomes an additional source of suffering imposed upon him by the enemies who surround him. "Save me, O God! For the waters have come up to my neck. . . . It is for your sake that I have borne reproach. . . . Zeal for your house has consumed me" (Ps. 69:1, 7, 9).

In the just man exposed to suffering, the memory of the disciples recognized Jesus: zeal for God's house leads him to the Passion, to the cross. This is the fundamental transformation that Jesus brought to the theme of zeal—*zēlos*. The "zeal" that would serve God through violence he transformed into the zeal of the cross. Thus he definitively established the criterion for true zeal—the zeal of self-giving love. This zeal must become the Christian's goal.

# Prayer

**St. Augustine**
*Confessions*

My good deeds are your act and your gift; my ill deeds are my own faults and your punishments. Let their breath come faster for the one, let them sigh for the other, and let the hymn of praise and the weeping rise up together in your sight from your censers which are the hearts of my brethren. And you, Lord, delighted with the odor of your holy temple, "have mercy upon me according to your great mercy" (Ps. 51:1), and for your name's sake; and in no point deserting what you have begun, supply what is imperfect in me.

Amen.

# Hymn

## *Cor, Arca Legem Continens*

**Latin**

*Cor, arca legem continens*
*Non servitutis veteris,*
*Sed gratiae, sed veniae,*
*Sed et misericordiae.*

*Cor, Sanctuarium novi*
*Intemeratum foederis,*
*Templum vetusto sanctius,*
*Velumque scisso utilius.*

*Te vulneratum caritas*
*Ictu patenti voluit;*
*Amoris invisibilis*
*Ut veneremur vulnera.*

*Hoc sub amoris symbolo*
*Passus cruenta, et mystica,*
*Utrumque sacrificium*
*Christus Sacerdos obtulit.*

**English**

Jesus, behind thy temple's veil,
Hid in an ark of gold,
On stones engraven, lay the Law
Thy finger wrote of old.

But in thy Body's Temple new,
Thy life-blood's throbbing shrine,
Held, upon fleshly tables graved,
The law of Love Divine.

And when that Heart in death was stilled,
Each temple's veil was riven:
And lo, within thy Love's red shrine,
To us to look was given.

There make us gaze and see the love
Which drew thee, for our sake,
O great high priest, thyself to God
A sacrifice to make.

*Quis non amantem redamet?*
*Quis non redemptus diligat,*
*Et Corde in isto seligat*
*Aeterna tabernacula?*

*Decus Parenti et Filio,*
*Sanctoque sit Spiritui,*
*Quibus potestas, gloria*
*Regnumque in omne est saeculum.*

Thou, Savior, cause that every soul
Which thou hast loved so well,
May will within thine open Heart
In life and death to dwell.

Grant it, O Father, only Son,
And Spirit, God of grace,
To whom all worship shall be done,
In every time and place.

# Reflection

**Pope Francis**
**Angelus**

This gesture of Jesus and his prophetic message are fully understood in the light of his Paschal Mystery. We have here, according to the evangelist John, the first proclamation of the death and Resurrection of Christ: His body, destroyed on the cross by the violence of sin, *will become in the Resurrection the universal meeting place between God and mankind.* And the Risen Christ is himself the universal meeting place—for everyone!—between God and mankind. For this reason, his humanity is the true temple where God is revealed, speaks, is encountered; and the true worshipers, the true worshipers of God are not only the guardians of the material temple, the keepers of power and of religious knowledge, [but] they are those *who worship God "in spirit and truth"* (John 4:23).

In this time of Lent we are preparing for the celebration of Easter, when we will renew the promises of our Baptism. Let us walk in the world as Jesus did, and let us make our whole existence a sign of our love for our brothers, especially the weakest and poorest; let us build for God a temple of our lives. And so we make it "encounterable" for those who we find along our journey. If we are witnesses of the Living Christ, so many people will encounter Jesus in us, in our witness. But, we ask—and each one of us can ask ourselves—does the Lord feel at home in my life? Do we allow him to "cleanse" our hearts and to drive out the idols, those attitudes of cupidity, jealousy, worldliness, envy, hatred, those habits of gossiping and tearing down others? Do I allow him to cleanse all the behaviors that are against God, against our neighbor, and against ourselves? . . .

Jesus never strikes. Jesus cleanses with tenderness, mercy, love. Mercy is his way of cleansing. Let us, each of us, let us allow the Lord to enter with his mercy—not with the whip, no, with his mercy—to cleanse our hearts. With us, Jesus' whip is his mercy. Let us open to him the gates so that he will make us a little purer.

# Poem

**Dante**
**From *Paradise***

So I beseech the Mind wherein your power
    and motion has its source, that you may turn
    to see the smoke that has obscured your fire,
And one more time grow angry and not brook
    selling and buying within that Temple gate—
    that Temple bricked with miracles and blood!

# Prayer

**St. Thérèse of Lisieux**
**From Homage to the Most Blessed Trinity**

O my God, behold us as we bow before you. We come to beseech you for the grace of working for your glory.

The blasphemies of sinners have sounded painfully in our ears. We wish to console you and to repair for the insults that souls redeemed by you make you suffer. . . . O my God! grant us the grace to be more vigilant in seeking sacrifices than those who do not love you are in their pursuit of worldly goods. . . .

O blessed Trinity, grant us to be faithful and give us the grace to possess you after the exile of this life.

Amen.

"In place of Solomon's temple, Christ has built a temple of living stones, the communion of saints. At its center, he stands as the eternal high priest; on its altar he is himself the perpetual sacrifice."

—EDITH STEIN
(ST. TERESA BENEDICTA OF THE CROSS)

# Tuesday *of* Holy Week

# THE HOUR
# HAS COME

# Scripture
**John 12:20–36**

Some Greeks who had come to worship at the Passover Feast came to Philip, who was from Bethsaida in Galilee, and asked him, "Sir, we would like to see Jesus." Philip went and told Andrew; then Andrew and Philip went and told Jesus. Jesus answered them, "The hour has come for the Son of Man to be glorified. Amen, amen, I say to you, unless a grain of wheat falls to the ground and dies, it remains just a grain of wheat; but if it dies, it produces much fruit. Whoever loves his life loses it, and whoever hates his life in this world will preserve it for eternal life. Whoever serves me must follow me, and where I am, there also will my servant be. The Father will honor whoever serves me.

"I am troubled now. Yet what should I say? 'Father, save me from this hour'? But it was for this purpose that I came to this hour. Father, glorify your name." Then a voice came from heaven, "I have glorified it and will glorify it again." The crowd there heard it and said it was thunder; but others said, "An angel has spoken to him." Jesus answered and said, "This voice did not come for my sake but for yours. Now is the time of judgment on this world; now the ruler of this world will be driven out. And when I am lifted up from the earth, I will draw everyone to myself." He said this indicating the kind of death he would die. So the crowd answered him, "We have heard from the law that the Messiah remains forever. Then how can you say that the Son of Man must be lifted up? Who is this Son of Man?" Jesus said to them, "The light will be among you only a little while. Walk while you have the light, so that darkness may not overcome you. Whoever walks in the dark does not know where he is going. While you have the light, believe in the light, so that you may become children of the light."

# Reading

**Bishop Barron**
*The Priority of Christ*

Jesus' "hour" is code for the Paschal Mystery, Jesus' passage through death to life. Pope Leo the Great gave voice to a patristic commonplace when he said in reference to Christ, "Nec alia fuit Dei Filio causa nascendi quam ut cruci possit affigi" (the reason for the birth of the Son of God was none other than that he might be fixed to a cross). In some more recent Christologies, it has been suggested that the death of Jesus was the result of merely social and political forces: the conservative establishment's resistance to his radical agenda; the Roman authorities' fear that his claim to kingship threatened their hegemony; the religious leaders' unwarranted concern that his language was blasphemous. The classical view that the death of Jesus was, in some sense, part of God's own purposes is, in these Christologies, either passed over in embarrassment or explicitly denied. But if we abandon the conviction that the death of Jesus was not simply a historical accident but an expression of God's intentionality, then we fly in the face of the overwhelming bulk of the tradition and of the New Testament itself. An interpreter would make a mockery of the Gospels were she to remove from the texture of the narrative the *dei*, the divinely grounded necessity of Jesus' going to the cross.

And were one to propose that the Pauline letters could be read on the supposition that the cross of Christ was merely the consequence of political forces, he would be running consistently against the grain of those texts.

We can begin to make sense of the providential necessity of the cross when we see Jesus' death in terms of the warrior icon. Because he is the incarnation of God's *ordo*, he has come to fight. He fights the most obvious forms of disorder as they appear in the political, cultural, and interpersonal realms, and he fights the powers and principalities—the spiritual forces—that undergird those more immediately apparent dysfunctions.

But his fighting will not be complete until he has conquered the final enemy, that which the powers use to do their work: the fear of death. That terror of final extinction is the cloud that broods over the whole of the apparatus of human misery, and so it is that terror that Jesus must face down. That he does so in accordance with his Father's will is thus perfectly consistent with the logic of the Incarnation: the bringing of the divine love to the darkest corners. The Passion narratives are the accounts of this ultimate battle, and this explains why they bristle with such enormous spiritual energy.

We hear in Luke 22, after his triumphant entry into Jerusalem and his cleansing of the temple, this ominous line: "The chief priests and the scribes were looking for a way to put Jesus to death, for they were afraid of the people" (Luke 22:2). We see here not only opposition but the particular form of opposition that is scapegoating. The leaders of the nation are seeking to isolate and eliminate Jesus because they are anxious to soothe tensions among the people. The author of John's Gospel stresses this dimension when he puts in the mouth of Caiaphas the words "You do not understand that it is better for you to have one man die for the people than to have the whole nation destroyed" (John 11:50). In Jesus, the true God will undermine this officially sanctioned scapegoating by becoming the scapegoat himself.

# Reflection

**Fulton Sheen**
*Life of Christ*

"The hour is now come for the Son of Man to achieve his glory" (John 12:23).

At Cana, our Lord had told his mother that his "hour" had not yet come; during his public ministry no man could lay hand on him because his "hour had not yet come"; but here he announced, within a few days of his death, that the time had come when he would be glorified. The glorification referred to the lowest depths of his humiliation on the cross, but it also referred to his triumph. He did not say the hour was near for him to die, but for him to be glorified. He grouped Calvary and his triumph together as he would do after his Resurrection when speaking to the disciples on the way to Emmaus: "Was it not to be expected that the Christ should undergo these sufferings, and enter so into his glory?" (Luke 24:26).

To his followers the cross presently seemed as the depth of humiliation; to him it was the height of glory.

# Prayer

**Thomas à Kempis**
*The Imitation of Christ*

Lord God, Holy Father, may you be blessed now and in eternity. For as you will, so is it done; and what you do is good. Let your servant rejoice in you—not in himself or in any other, for you alone are true joy. You are my hope and my crown. You, O Lord, are my joy and my honor.

What does your servant possess that he has not received from you, and that without any merit of his own? Yours are all the things which you have given, all the things which you have made.

I am poor and in labors since my youth, and my soul is sorrowful sometimes even to the point of tears. At times, also, my spirit is troubled because of impending sufferings. I long for the joy of peace. Earnestly I beg for the peace of your children who are fed by you in the light of consolation. If you give peace, if you infuse holy joy, the soul of your servant shall be filled with holy song and be devout in praising you. But if you withdraw yourself, as you so very often do, he will not be able to follow the way of your commandments, but will rather be obliged to strike his breast and bend the knee, because his today is different from yesterday and the day before when your light shone upon his head and he was protected in the shadow of your wings from the temptations rushing upon him.

Just Father, ever to be praised, the hour is come for your servant to be tried. Beloved Father, it is right that in this hour your servant should suffer something for you. O Father, forever to be honored, the hour which you knew from all eternity is at hand, when for a short time your servant should be outwardly oppressed, but inwardly should ever live with you.

Let him be a little slighted, let him be humbled, let him fail in the sight of men, let him be afflicted with sufferings and pains, so that he may rise again with you in the dawn of the new light and be glorified in heaven.

Amen.

# Hymn

*Vexilla Regis Prodeunt*

**Latin**

*Vexilla Regis prodeunt:*
*Fulget Crucis mysterium,*
*Qua vita mortem pertulit,*
*Et morte vitam protulit.*

*Quae vulnerata lanceae*
*Mucrone diro, criminum*
*Ut nos lavaret sordibus,*
*Manavit unda, et sanguine.*

*Impleta sunt quae concinit*
*David fideli carmine,*
*Dicendo nationibus:*
*Regnavit a ligno Deus.*

*Arbor decora et fulgida,*
*Ornata regis purpura,*
*Electa digno stipite*
*Tarn sancta membra tangere.*

## English

Abroad the regal banners fly,
Now shines the cross' mystery;
Upon it Life did death endure,
And yet by death did life procure.

Who, wounded with a direful spear,
Did, purposely to wash us clear
From stain of sin, pour out a flood
Of precious Water mixed with Blood.

That which the Prophet-King of old
Hath in mysterious verse foretold,
Is now accomplished, whilst we see
God ruling nations from a Tree.

O lovely and refulgent Tree,
Adorned with purpled majesty;
Culled from a worthy stock, to bear
Those Limbs which sanctified were.

*Beata, cuius brachiis*
*Pretium pependit saeculi,*
*Statera facta corporis,*
*Tulitque praedam tartari.*

*O Crux ave spes unica,*
*Hoc passionis tempore*
*Piis adauge gratiam,*
*Reisque dele crimina.*

*Te, fons salutis Trinitas,*
*Collaudet omnis spiritus:*
*Quibus Crucis victoriam*
*Largiris, adde praemium.*

Blest Tree, whose happy branches bore
The wealth that did the world restore;
The beam that did that Body weigh
Which raised up hell's expected prey.

Hail, cross, of hopes the most sublime!
Now in this mournful Passion time,
Improve religious souls in grace,
The sins of criminals efface.

Blest Trinity, salvation's spring,
May every soul thy praises sing;
To those thou grantest conquest by
The Holy Cross, rewards apply.

# Reflection

**St. Elizabeth of the Trinity**
**Letter**

Rejoice in the thought that from all eternity we have been known of the Father, as St. Paul says, and that he wishes to find in us the image of his crucified Son. If you knew how necessary suffering is in order that God's work may be done in the soul! The good God has an immense desire to enrich us with his graces, but it is we who determine the amount in proportion as we allow ourselves to be immolated by him—immolated, like the Master, in joy, in thanksgiving, saying with him: "The chalice which my Father hath given, shall I not drink it?" (John 18:11).

He called the hour of his Passion "his hour," that for which he had come, that for which he yearned with all his strength. When a great suffering, or a very small sacrifice is offered us, let us think quickly that it is "our hour," the hour to prove our love for him who, as St. Paul says, loved us exceedingly.

# Poem

**Paul Claudel**
**From "Stations of the Cross"**

O see, my soul, and fear! Pregnant the solemn hour
When the eternal wood first pressed the Son of God.
Then Eden's tree full-grown bore fruit in Paradise.
Behold, O sinful soul, the end thy sin has served.
God triumphs over crime; on every cross hangs Christ.
The sin of man is great; but we are silent, mute.
Heaven's conquering God debates not, but fulfills.

Jesus accepts the cross as we receive Himself.
As Jeremiah said we give Him wood for food.
How huge that awful cross; how cumbersome and large;
Unyielding, painful, hard, a senseless sinner's weight.
To bear it step by step till one shall die thereon!
Dost Thou go forth to bear it, Saviour Christ, alone?

With patience may I bear what share Thou givest me.
Each one must bear the cross ere cross his comfort be.

# Prayer

St. Thérèse of Lisieux
**Prayer Inspired by an Image of St. Joan of Arc**

Lord, God of hosts, in the Gospel you told us: "I have not come to bring peace but the sword" (Matt. 10:34). Arm me for battle; I burn to fight for your glory but I beg you to strengthen my courage. . . . Then with Holy King David I can exclaim:

"You alone are my sword, you, Lord train my hands for war" (see Ps. 144:1). . . . O my Beloved! I know what combat you have in mind for me; the contest will not be on the field of battle. . . .

I am a prisoner of your Love. I have freely forged the chain that binds me to you and separates me forever from that world which you have cursed. . . . My sword is nothing but Love—with it I will chase the foreigner from the kingdom. I will have you proclaimed King in the souls who refuse to submit to your Divine Power.

Doubtless, Lord, you do not need such a feeble instrument as myself, but Joan, your chaste and courageous bride, said: "We must fight so that God may give the victory." O my Jesus, I will fight then, for your Love, until the evening of my life. As you did not wish to rest on earth, I want to follow your example. I hope this promise that fell from your Divine lips will find fulfillment in me: "If anyone follow me, where

I am, there also will my servant be. Whoever serves me, my Father will honor" (John 12:26).

To be with you, to be in you is my one desire. . . . This assurance that you give me of its fulfillment helps me to bear my exile while awaiting the glorious day of the eternal Face to Face!

Amen.

"He was awaiting this hour, not fated, but suitable and self-chosen that all things might first be fulfilled which should be fulfilled before his Passion."

—ST. AUGUSTINE

# Wednesday *of* Holy Week

# THE BETRAYAL

# Scripture
**Luke 22:3–6**

Then Satan entered into Judas, the one surnamed Iscariot, who was counted among the Twelve, and he went to the chief priests and temple guards to discuss a plan for handing him over to them. They were pleased and agreed to pay him money. He accepted their offer and sought a favorable opportunity to hand him over to them in the absence of a crowd.

# Reading

**Bishop Barron**
*And Now I See*

The Greek word *paradidonai* (to hand over, to betray) appears numerous times and in various grammatical forms in the Passion accounts: the temple guards *hand him over* to the Sanhedrin who *hand him over* to Pilate who *hands him over* to be scourged and who finally *hands him over* to be crucified. Throughout the events leading up to his death, Jesus is tossed around like a plaything, becoming increasingly passive and silent, incapable of disposing of himself. Here, he enters into the spiritual and psychological world of the sinner. Having lost the link to the divine, the sinner is without anchor, "tossed about" from influence to influence, from person to person, never able confidently to take hold of his life. Jesus identifies with this splintered consciousness as he is repeatedly "betrayed."

But there is something even stranger and more awful at work here. The ultimate betrayer of Jesus is neither Judas nor the high priest nor the Sanhedrin nor the Romans, but rather the Father. If Jesus is the one sent by the Father to go into the godforsakenness of the sinner, then the Father "rejects" him, turns his back on him, delivers him over to his torturers and murderers. In the terrible language of Scripture, God does not "spare" his only Son but gives him over for our sake (Rom. 8:32). Just as in the Old Testament narratives, Yahweh delivered Israel over to its enemies on account of its sins, so the Father delivers over the Son who "becomes" sin (see 2 Cor. 5:21). Jesus himself signals the priority of the Father's handing over in his dialogue with Pilate. The Roman governor, in a menacing tone, reminds the helpless criminal that he has the power to release him or crucify him, and Jesus laconically replies that Pilate would have no power over him unless it had been granted "from above" (John 19:11). The earthly betrayers are, in the deepest sense, but the agents of the Father's desire that the Son go into godforsakenness. We must not, of course, literalize this symbol in an emotional direction, as if the Father hates the Son, engaging in a sort of divine child abuse. On the contrary, we see in this motif of divine "betrayal" the willingness of God to break his own heart out of love, to enter personally into the experience of being alienated from God.

# Reflection

**Origen**

*Commentary on Matthew*

Judas means "confessor." Luke the Evangelist numbers both "Judas the son of James and Judas Iscariot" among the twelve Apostles (Luke 6:16). Since two of Christ's disciples were given this same name and since there can be no meaningless symbol in the Christian mystery, I am convinced that the two Judases represent two distinct types of confessing Christians.

The first, symbolized by Judas the son of James, perseveres in remaining faithful to Christ. The second type, however, after once believing and professing faith in Christ, then abandons him out of greed. He defects to the heretics and to the false priests of the Jews, that is, to counterfeit Christians, and (insofar as he is able) delivers Christ, the "Word of truth," over to them to be crucified and destroyed. This type of Christian is represented by Judas Iscariot, who "went out to the chief priests" (Matt. 26:14) and agreed on a price for betraying Christ.

# Prayer

**St. Catherine of Siena**

*The Dialogue*

Immeasurable Love! . . . You would have me know myself and your goodness, and the sins committed against you by every class of people and especially by your ministers, so that I might draw tears from the knowledge of your infinite goodness and let them flow as a river over my wretched self and over these wretched living dead. Therefore it is my will, ineffable Fire, joyous Love, eternal Father, that my desire should never weary of longing for your honor and the salvation of souls. And I beg you, let my eyes never rest, but in your grace make of them two rivers for the water that flows from you, the sea of peace. . . .

Oh, you are a good shepherd to have given us your only-begotten Son to be our true shepherd who in obedience to you laid down his life for your little sheep (John 10:11) and made of his blood a bath for us. It is this blood that your servants, hungry as they are, are asking for at this door. They are asking you through this blood to be merciful to the world and make holy Church blossom again with the fragrant flowers of good holy shepherds whose perfume will dispel the stench of the putrid evil flowers.

You said, eternal Father, that because of your love for your creatures, and through the prayers and innocent sufferings of your servants, you would be merciful to the world and reform holy Church, and thus give us refreshment. Do not wait any longer, then, to turn the eye of your mercy. Because it is your will to answer us before we call, answer now with the voice of your mercy.

Open the door of your immeasurable charity, which you have given us in the door of the Word (see John 10:7). Yes, I know that you open before we knock, because your servants knock and call out to you with the very love and affection you gave them, seeking your honor and the salvation of souls. Give them then the bread of life, the fruit of the blood of your only-begotten Son, which they are begging of you for the glory and praise of your name and for the salvation of souls. For it would seem you would receive more glory and praise by saving so many people than by letting them stubbornly persist in their hardness. To you, eternal Father, everything is possible. Though you created us without our help, it is not your will to save us without our help. So I beg you to force their wills and dispose them to want what they do not want. I ask this of your infinite mercy. You created us out of nothing. So, now that we exist, be merciful and remake the vessels you created and formed in your image and likeness; re-form them to grace in the mercy and blood of your Son.

Amen.

# Hymn

*Miserere Mei, Deus*
(Psalm 51)

**Latin**

*Miserere mei, Deus, secundum magnam*
*misericordiam tuam;*
*et secundum multitudinem miserationum*
*tuarum, dele iniquitatem meam.*
*Amplius lava me ab iniquitate mea,*
*et a peccato meo munda me.*

*Quoniam iniquitatem meam ego cognosco,*
*et peccatum meum contra me est semper.*
*Tibi soli peccavi, et malum coram te feci;*

*ut iustificeris in sermonibus tuis,*
*et vincas cum iudicaris.*
*Ecce enim in iniquitatibus conceptus sum,*
*et in peccatis concepit me mater mea.*

## English

Have mercy on me, God, in your kindness.
In your compassion blot out my offense.
O wash me more and more from my guilt
and cleanse me from my sin.


My offenses truly I know them;
my sin is always before me.
Against you, you alone, have I sinned;
what is evil in your sight I have done.

That you may be justified when you give sentence
and be without reproach when you judge.
O see, in guilt I was born,
a sinner was I conceived.

*Ecce enim veritatem dilexisti;*
*incerta et occulta sapientiae tuae manifestasti mihi.*
*Asperges me hyssopo, et mundabor;*
*lavabis me, et super nivem dealbabor.*

*Auditui meo dabis gaudium et laetitiam,*
*et exsultabunt ossa humiliata.*
*Averte faciem tuam a peccatis meis,*
*et omnes iniquitates meas dele.*

*Cor mundum crea in me, Deus,*
*et spiritum rectum innova in visceribus meis.*
*Ne proiicias me a facie tua,*
*et spiritum sanctum tuum ne auferas a me.*

*Redde mihi laetitiam salutaris tui,*
*et spiritu principali confirma me.*
*Docebo iniquos vias tuas,*
*et impii ad te convertentur.*
*Libera me de sanguinibus, Deus,*

*Deus salutis meae,*
*et exsultabit lingua mea iustitiam tuam.*
*Domine, labia mea aperies,*
*et os meum annuntiabit laudem tuam.*

Indeed you love truth in the heart;
then in the secret of my heart teach me wisdom.
O purify me, then I shall be clean;
O wash me, I shall be whiter than snow.

Make me hear rejoicing and gladness,
that the bones you have crushed may revive.
From my sins turn away your face
and blot out all my guilt.

A pure heart create for me, O God,
put a steadfast spirit within me.
Do not cast me away from your presence,
nor deprive me of your holy spirit.

Give me again the joy of your help;
with a spirit of fervor sustain me,
that I may teach transgressors your ways
and sinners may return to you.

O rescue me, God, my helper,
and my tongue shall ring out your goodness.
O Lord, open my lips
and my mouth shall declare your praise.

*Quoniam si voluisses sacrificium, dedissem utique;*
*holocaustis non delectaberis.*
*Sacrificium Deo spiritus contribulatus;*
*cor contritum et humiliatum, Deus, non despicies.*

*Benigne fac, Domine, in bona voluntate tua Sion,*
*ut aedificentur muri Ierusalem.*
*Tunc acceptabis sacrificium iustitiae,*
*oblationes et holocausta;*
*tunc imponent super altare tuum vitulos.*

For in sacrifice you take no delight,
burnt offering from me you would refuse,
my sacrifice, a contrite spirit.
A humbled, contrite heart you will not spurn.

In your goodness, show favor to Zion:
rebuild the walls of Jerusalem.
Then you will be pleased with lawful sacrifice,
holocausts offered on your altar.

# Reflection

**St. Jerome**
**Letter**

In the lives of Christians we look not to the beginnings but to the endings. Paul began badly but ended well. The start of Judas wins praise; his end is condemned because of his treachery. Read Ezekiel, "The righteousness of the righteous shall not deliver him in the day of his transgression; as for the wickedness of the wicked he shall not fall thereby in the day that he turns from his wickedness" (Ezek. 33:12). The Christian life is the true Jacob's ladder on which the angels ascend and descend (Gen. 28:12), while the Lord stands above it holding out his hand to those who slip and sustaining by the vision of himself the weary steps of those who ascend.

# Poem

**Thomas Merton**
"The Betrayal"


The sense that sits in the thin skins of lips
Was waiting with a traitor's kiss that made You sweat
    with death,
When envy, in the Lenten night,
Shone sharp as lightnings: and we came with blades.


What hate, what worlds of wormwood did our tongues
    distill!
We cried with voices dry as shot,
In Pilate's yard where pride of life
And love of glory laced Your brows in Blood.


What were our curses, dark as vinegar,
We swore, with tongues as sharp as thongs,
On Golgotha, where pride of life,
With easy slanders nailed You to the wood!


And all we uttered, all, was nails and gall,
With our desires cruel as steel.
We digged Your hands, and filled them full of Blood.
With little smiles as dry as dice
We whipped and killed You for Your lovely world.

You died, and paid Your traitors with a prayer
And cured our swearing darkness with Your wounds'
    five lights.
Eyes see Your holy hands, and, in them, flowers.
You let the doubter's finger feel the sun in Your side,
Ears have Your words, and tongues believe You wheat:
You feed with life the lips that kissed You dead!

# Prayer

**St. Thérèse of Lisieux**
*Story of a Soul*

The King of the Fatherland of the bright sun actually came and lived for thirty-three years in the land of darkness. Alas! the darkness did not understand that this Divine King was the Light of the world.

Your child, however, O Lord, has understood your divine light, and she begs pardon for her brothers. She is resigned to eat the bread of sorrow as long as you desire it; she does not wish to rise up from this table filled with bitterness at which poor sinners are eating until the day set by you. Can she not say in her name and in the name of her brothers, "Have pity on us, O Lord, for we are poor sinners!" Oh! Lord, send us away justified. May all those who were not enlightened by the bright flame of faith one day see it shine. O Jesus! if it is needful that the table soiled by them be purified by a soul who loves you, then I desire to eat this bread of trial at this table until it pleases you to bring me into your bright Kingdom. The only grace I ask of you is that I never offend you!

Amen.

"He is sold, and very cheap, for it is only for thirty pieces of silver; but he redeems the world, and that at a great price, for the price was his own blood."

—ST. GREGORY NAZIANZEN

# Holy Thursday

# THE LAST SUPPER

# Scripture
## Luke 22:7–20

When the day of the feast of Unleavened Bread arrived, the day for sacrificing the Passover lamb, he sent out Peter and John, instructing them, "Go and make preparations for us to eat the Passover." They asked him, "Where do you want us to make the preparations?" And he answered them, "When you go into the city, a man will meet you carrying a jar of water. Follow him into the house that he enters and say to the master of the house, 'The teacher says to you, "Where is the guest room where I may eat the Passover with my disciples?"' He will show you a large upper room that is furnished. Make the preparations there." Then they went off and found everything exactly as he had told them, and there they prepared the Passover.

When the hour came, Jesus took his place at table with the apostles. He said to them, "I have eagerly desired to eat this Passover with you before I suffer, for, I tell you, I shall not eat it again until there is fulfillment in the kingdom of God." Then he took a cup, gave thanks, and said, "Take this and share it among yourselves; for I tell you that from this time on I shall not drink of the fruit of the vine until the kingdom of God comes." Then he took the bread, said the blessing, broke it, and gave it to them, saying, "This is my body, which will be given for you; do this in memory of me."

And likewise the cup after they had eaten, saying, "This cup is the new covenant in my blood, which will be shed for you."

# Reading
**Bishop Barron**
*Eucharist*

Jesus was using the Passover supper to give a definitive interpretation to the actions that he would take the next day, Good Friday. As this bread is broken and shared, so, he was saying, my body tomorrow will be broken and offered; as this cup is poured out, so my blood tomorrow will be poured out in sacrifice. His body, he was implying, will be like the animals offered by Abraham when God struck a covenant with him, and his blood will be like the oxen's blood sprinkled by Moses on the altar and on the people, sealing the agreement of the Torah. In his crucified body, he will be like the Passover lamb slaughtered in the temple, signifying Israel's total commitment to Yahweh and Yahweh's to Israel. Moreover, his body will be like that of Isaac as he waited for the knife of his father to fall, with the telling difference that Jesus' Father will carry through the sacrifice.

And if we attend carefully to the words over the cup, we can't help but see that his act on the cross will be the condition for the possibility of the perfect covenant of which Jeremiah dreamed (Jer. 31:33). When Jesus said, "This cup that is poured out for you is the new covenant in my blood" (Luke 22:20), his disciples certainly thought of the promise that one day Yahweh would effect a fully realized union with his people. And when they heard that this covenant was to be accompanied by the shedding of blood, how could they not think of the link between Jeremiah's dream and the suffering servant of Isaiah?

In sum, the words of Jesus over the bread and cup at the Last Supper effected a stunning gathering of the variety of strands of covenantal and sacrificial theology in the Hebrew Scriptures. The covenants and their accompanying sacrifices that mark the entire religious history of the Jews are being recapitulated, Jesus says, in me and my sacrifice. He undoubtedly knew that the horror of the Crucifixion would be so stark as to block any attempt to assign meaning to it. And thus, in the relative safety and intimacy of the upper room, Jesus calmly and in advance provided the interpretive key to the climactic action of his life.

Why did Jesus invite his disciples to consume the bread and wine that he had radically identified with his sacrifice? In Jeremiah's prophecy of the new covenant, Yahweh had said, "I will put my law within them, and I will write it on their hearts" (Jer. 31:33). This means that the everlasting agreement would be written not on stone tablets but in the flesh of the people's hearts; it would not be an oppressive law externally imposed but a rule congruent with the deepest longing of the human soul. Jesus thus wanted them to ingest his sacrifice so as to appropriate it in the most intimate, organic way, making it bone of their bone and flesh of their flesh. Thomas Aquinas commented that the old Law of the Torah and the various covenants had a mitigated effectiveness, precisely because it appeared as external to the human heart. But, he continued, the new Law of the Gospel is efficacious because it is realized internally, through the identification of Christ and his Body the Church. And nowhere is this identification more complete than in the Eucharist, when a disciple physically consumes the incarnate Christ, the Law par excellence.

# Reflection

**St. Ambrose**
*On the Mysteries*

The Lord Jesus himself proclaims: "This is my body" (Matt. 26:26). Before the blessing of the heavenly words another nature is spoken of; after the consecration the Body is signified. He himself speaks of his Blood. Before the consecration it has another name; after it is called Blood. And you say, Amen, that is, it is true. Let the heart within confess what the mouth utters; let the soul feel what the voice speaks.

Christ, then, feeds his Church with these sacraments, by means of which the substance of the soul is strengthened; the Church, beholding so great grace, exhorts her sons and her friends to come together to the sacraments, saying: "Eat, my friends, and drink and be inebriated, my brother" (Song of Sol. 5:1). What we eat and what we drink the Holy Spirit has elsewhere made plain by the prophet, saying, "Taste and see that the Lord is good; blessed is the man that hopes in him" (Ps. 34:8). In that sacrament is Christ; because it is the Body of Christ, it is therefore not bodily food but spiritual.

# Prayer

**St. Alphonsus de Liguori**

*Visits to the Most Holy Sacrament and to Most Holy Mary*

My sacramental Savior, O divine lover, how lovely the tender inventions of your love to make yourself loved by others! O Eternal Word, having become man, you were not content simply to die for us. You have also given us this Sacrament as company, as food, and as a pledge of paradise. You make yourself appear among us, first as a child in a stable, then as a poor man in a workshop, then as a criminal on a cross, and now as bread on an altar. . . .

My beloved Redeemer, you have spent all your life on me. And what have I to love, if not you who are all beautiful, all kind, all good, all loving, all gracious? My soul lives only to love you.

Amen.

# Hymn

*Pange Lingua Gloriosi Corporis Mysterium*
(with *Tantum Ergo*)

## Latin

*Pange, lingua, gloriosi*
*corporis mysterium,*
*sanguinisque pretiosi,*
*quem in mundi pretium*
*fructus ventris generosi*
*rex effudit gentium.*

*Nobis datus, nobis natus*
*ex intacta Virgine,*
*et in mundo conversatus,*
*sparso verbi semine,*
*sui moras incolatus*
*miro clausit ordine.*

*In supremae nocte coenae*
*recumbens cum fratribus,*
*observata lege plene*
*cibis in legalibus,*
*cibum turbae duodenae*
*se dat suis manibus.*

## English

Sing, my tongue, the Savior's glory,
of his flesh the mystery sing,
of the blood, all price exceeding,
shed by our immortal king,
destined for the world's redemption,
from a noble womb to spring.

Given for us, and condescending,
to be born for us below,
high with lowly converse blending
far the seed of truth to sow,
till he died with wondrous ending,
bearing all our weight of woe.

At that last great supper lying,
circled by his chosen band,
humbly with the law complying,
first he finished its command,
then immortal food supplying,
gave himself with his own hand.

*Verbum caro panem verum,*
*Verbo carnem efficit;*
*fitque sanguis Christi merum:*
*et si sensus deficit,*
*ad firmandum cor sincerum*
*sola fides sufficit.*

*Tantum ergo sacramentum*
*veneremur cernui,*
*et antiquum documentum*
*novo cedat ritui,*
*praestet fides supplementum*
*sensuum defectui.*

*Genitori genitoque*
*laus et iubilatio,*
*salus, honor, virtus quoque*
*sit et benedictio,*
*procedenti ab utroque*
*compar sit laudatio.*

Word-made-flesh, the bread of nature,
by his Word to Flesh he turns;
wine into his Blood he changes
though our sense no change discerns.
But, if inmost heart be earnest,
faith her lesson quickly learns.

Therefore, we, before him bending,
this great sacrament revere;
types and shadows have their ending,
for the newer rite is here;
faith, our outward sense befriending,
makes our inward vision clear.

Glory, let us give, and blessing
to the Father and the Son,
honor, might, and praise addressing
while eternal ages run;
ever, too, his love confessing,
who, from both, with both is one.

# Reflection

## Pope Benedict XVI

*Jesus of Nazareth: Part Two: Holy Week*

"When they had sung a hymn, they went out to the Mount of Olives." With these words, Matthew and Mark conclude their accounts of the Last Supper (Matt. 26:30; Mark 14:26). Jesus' final meal—whether or not it was a Passover meal—was first and foremost an act of worship. At its heart was the prayer of praise and thanksgiving, and at the end it led back into prayer. Still praying, Jesus goes out into the night with his disciples, reminding us of the night when the first-born of Egypt were struck down and Israel was saved through the blood of the lamb (see Exod. 12). Jesus goes out into the night during which he will have to take upon himself the destiny of the lamb. . . .

This is one of the most venerable sites of Christianity. True, the trees do not date from the time of Jesus; Titus cut down all the trees within a wide radius during the siege of Jerusalem. Yet it is still the same Mount of Olives. Anyone who spends time here is confronted with one of the most dramatic moments in the mystery of our Savior: it was here that Jesus experienced that final loneliness, the whole anguish of the human condition. Here the abyss of sin and evil penetrated deep within his soul. Here he was to quake with foreboding of his imminent death. Here he was kissed

by the betrayer. Here he was abandoned by all the disciples.
Here he wrestled with his destiny for my sake.


# Poem
**Gerard Manley Hopkins**
**"Easter Communion"**


Pure fasted faces draw unto this feast:
God comes all sweetness to your Lenten lips.
You striped in secret with breath-taking whips,
Those crooked rough-scored chequers may be pieced
To crosses meant for Jesu's; you whom the East
With draught of thin and pursuant cold so nips
Breathe Easter now; you serged fellowships,
You vigil-keepers with low flames decreased,

God shall o'er-brim the measures you have spent
With oil of gladness, for sackcloth and frieze
And the ever-fretting shirt of punishment
Give myrrhy-threaded golden folds of ease.
Your scarce-sheathed bones are weary of being bent:
Lo, God shall strengthen all the feeble knees.

# Prayer

**St. Thérèse of Lisieux**

**From the Prayer for Acquiring Humility**

O Jesus! when you were a Pilgrim on earth, you said: "Learn of me for I am gentle and humble of heart and you will find rest for your souls" (Matt. 11:29). O Mighty Monarch of Heaven, yes, my soul finds rest in seeing you, clothed in the form and nature of a slave, humbling yourself to wash the feet of your Apostles. I recall your words that teach me how to practice humility: "I have given you an example so that you may do what I have done. The disciple is not greater than the Master. . . . If you understand this, happy are you if you put them into practice" (John 13:15–17).

Lord, I do understand these words that came from your gentle and humble Heart and I want to practice them with the help of your grace. I want truly to humble myself. . . .

Now in the Sacred Host I see you at the height of your annihilations. How humble you are, O divine King of Glory, to subject yourself to all your priests without making any distinction between those who love you and those who are, alas! lukewarm or cold in your service. . . . At their word you come down from heaven. Whether they advance or delay the hour of the Holy Sacrifice, you are always ready. . . .

O my Beloved, how gentle and humble of heart you seem under the veil of the white Host! To teach me humility you cannot humble yourself further. . . .

I beg you, my Divine Jesus, to send me a humiliation whenever I try to set myself above others. I know, O my God, that you humble the proud soul but to the one who humbles herself you give an eternity of glory. So I want to put myself in the last rank and to share your humiliations so as "to have a share with you" in the kingdom of heaven.

Amen.

"I want the Bread of God which is the Flesh of Christ, who was of the seed of David; and for drink I desire his Blood which is love that cannot be destroyed."

—ST. IGNATIUS OF ANTIOCH

# Good Friday

# THE PASSION AND CROSS

# Scripture
## John 18–19

Jesus went out with his disciples across the Kidron valley to where there was a garden, into which he and his disciples entered. Judas his betrayer also knew the place, because Jesus had often met there with his disciples. So Judas got a band of soldiers and guards from the chief priests and the Pharisees and went there with lanterns, torches, and weapons. Jesus, knowing everything that was going to happen to him, went out and said to them, "Whom are you looking for?" They answered him, "Jesus the Nazorean." He said to them, "I AM." Judas his betrayer was also with them. When he said to them, "I AM," they turned away and fell to the ground. So he again asked them, "Whom are you looking for?" They said, "Jesus the Nazorean." Jesus answered, "I told you that I AM. So if you are looking for me, let these men go." This was to fulfill what he had said, "I have not lost any of those you gave me." Then Simon Peter, who had a sword, drew it, struck the high priest's slave, and cut off his right ear. The slave's name was Malchus. Jesus said to Peter, "Put your sword into its scabbard. Shall I not drink the cup that the Father gave me?"

So the band of soldiers, the tribune, and the Jewish guards seized Jesus, bound him, and brought him to Annas first. He was the father-in-law of Caiaphas, who was high priest that year. It was Caiaphas who had counseled the Jews that it was better that one man should die rather than the people.

Simon Peter and another disciple followed Jesus. Now the other disciple was known to the high priest, and he entered the courtyard of the high priest with Jesus. But Peter stood at the gate outside. So the other disciple, the acquaintance of the high priest, went out and spoke to the gatekeeper and brought Peter in. Then the maid who was the gatekeeper said to Peter, "You are not one of this man's disciples, are you?" He said, "I am not." Now the slaves and the guards were standing around a charcoal fire that they had made, because it was cold, and were warming themselves. Peter was also standing there keeping warm.

The high priest questioned Jesus about his disciples and about his doctrine. Jesus answered him, "I have spoken publicly to the world. I have always taught in a synagogue or in the temple area where all the Jews gather, and in secret I have said nothing. Why ask me? Ask those who heard me what I said to them. They know what I said." When he had said this, one of the temple guards standing there struck Jesus and said, "Is this the way you answer the high priest?" Jesus answered him, "If I have spoken wrongly, testify to the wrong; but if I have spoken rightly, why do you strike me?" Then Annas sent him bound to Caiaphas the high priest.

Now Simon Peter was standing there keeping warm. And they said to him, "You are not one of his disciples, are you?" He denied it and said, "I am not." One of the slaves of the high priest, a relative of the one whose ear Peter had cut off, said, "Didn't I see you in the garden with him?" Again Peter denied it. And immediately the cock crowed.

Then they brought Jesus from Caiaphas to the praetorium. It was morning. And they themselves did not enter the praetorium, in order not to be defiled so that they could eat the Passover. So Pilate came out to them and said, "What charge do you bring against this man?" They answered and said to him, "If he were not a criminal, we would not have handed him over to you." At this, Pilate said to them, "Take him yourselves, and judge him according to your law." The Jews answered him, "We do not have the right to execute anyone," in order that the word of Jesus might be fulfilled that he said indicating the kind of death he would die. So Pilate went back into the praetorium and summoned Jesus and said to him, "Are you the King of the Jews?" Jesus answered, "Do you say this on your own or have others told you about me?" Pilate answered, "I am not a Jew, am I? Your own nation and the chief priests handed you over to me. What have you done?" Jesus answered, "My kingdom does not belong to this world. If my kingdom did belong to this world, my attendants would be fighting to keep me from being handed over to the Jews. But as it is, my kingdom is not here." So

Pilate said to him, "Then you are a king?" Jesus answered, "You say I am a king. For this I was born and for this I came into the world, to testify to the truth. Everyone who belongs to the truth listens to my voice." Pilate said to him, "What is truth?"

When he had said this, he again went out to the Jews and said to them, "I find no guilt in him. But you have a custom that I release one prisoner to you at Passover. Do you want me to release to you the King of the Jews?" They cried out again, "Not this one but Barabbas!" Now Barabbas was a revolutionary.

Then Pilate took Jesus and had him scourged. And the soldiers wove a crown out of thorns and placed it on his head, and clothed him in a purple cloak, and they came to him and said, "Hail, King of the Jews!" And they struck him repeatedly. Once more Pilate went out and said to them, "Look, I am bringing him out to you, so that you may know that I find no guilt in him." So Jesus came out, wearing the crown of thorns and the purple cloak. And he said to them, "Behold, the man!" When the chief priests and the guards saw him they cried out, "Crucify him, crucify him!" Pilate said to them, "Take him yourselves and crucify him. I find no guilt in him." The Jews answered, "We have a law, and according to that law he ought to die, because he made himself the Son of God." Now when Pilate heard this statement, he became even more afraid, and went back into the praetorium and said to Jesus, "Where are you from?" Jesus did not answer him. So Pilate said to him, "Do you not speak to me? Do you not know that I have power to release you and I have power to crucify you?" Jesus answered him, "You would have no power over me if it had not been given to you from above. For this reason the one who handed me over to you has the greater sin." Consequently, Pilate tried to release him; but the Jews cried out, "If you release him, you are not a Friend of Caesar. Everyone who makes himself a king opposes Caesar."

When Pilate heard these words he brought Jesus out and seated him on the judge's bench in the place called Stone Pavement, in Hebrew, Gabbatha. It was preparation day for Passover, and it was about noon. And he said to the Jews, "Behold, your king!" They cried out, "Take him away, take him away! Crucify him!" Pilate said to them, "Shall I crucify your king?" The chief priests answered, "We have no king but Caesar." Then he handed him over to them to be crucified.

So they took Jesus, and, carrying the cross himself, he went out to what is called the Place of the Skull, in Hebrew, Golgotha. There they crucified him, and with him two others, one on either side, with Jesus in the middle. Pilate also had an inscription written and put on the cross. It read, "Jesus the Nazorean, the King of the Jews." Now many of the Jews read this inscription, because the place where Jesus was crucified was near the city; and it was written in Hebrew, Latin, and Greek. So the chief priests of the Jews said to Pilate, "Do not write 'The King of the Jews,' but that he said, 'I am the King of the Jews'." Pilate answered, "What I have written, I have written."

When the soldiers had crucified Jesus, they took his clothes and divided them into four shares, a share for each soldier. They also took his tunic, but the tunic was seamless, woven in one piece from the top down. So they said to one another, "Let's not tear it, but cast lots for it to see whose it will be," in order that the passage of Scripture might be fulfilled that says:

*They divided my garments among them,*
*and for my vesture they cast lots.*

This is what the soldiers did. Standing by the cross of Jesus were his mother and his mother's sister, Mary the wife of Clopas, and Mary of Magdala. When Jesus saw his mother and the disciple there whom he loved he said to his mother, "Woman, behold, your son." Then he said to the disciple, "Behold, your mother." And from that hour the disciple took her into his home.

After this, aware that everything was now finished, in order that the Scripture might be fulfilled, Jesus said, "I thirst." There was a vessel filled with common wine. So they put a sponge soaked in wine on a sprig of hyssop and put it up to his mouth. When Jesus had taken the wine, he said, "It is finished." And bowing his head, he handed over the spirit.

*Here all kneel and pause for a short time.*

Now since it was preparation day, in order that the bodies might not remain on the cross on the sabbath, for the sabbath day of that week was a solemn one, the Jews asked Pilate that their legs be broken and that they be taken down. So the soldiers came and broke the legs of the first and then of the other one who was crucified with Jesus. But when they came to Jesus and saw that he was already dead, they did not break his legs, but one soldier thrust his lance into his side, and immediately blood and water flowed out. An eyewitness has testified, and his testimony is true; he knows that he is speaking the truth, so that you also may come to believe. For this happened so that the Scripture passage might be fulfilled:

*Not a bone of it will be broken.*

And again another passage says:

*They will look upon him whom they have pierced.*

After this, Joseph of Arimathea, secretly a disciple of Jesus for fear of the Jews, asked Pilate if he could remove the body of Jesus. And Pilate permitted it. So he came and took his body. Nicodemus, the one who had first come to him at night, also came bringing a mixture of myrrh and aloes weighing about one hundred pounds. They took the body of Jesus and bound it with burial cloths along with the spices, according to the Jewish burial custom. Now in the place where he had been crucified there was a garden, and in the garden a new tomb, in which no one had yet been buried. So they laid Jesus there because of the Jewish preparation day; for the tomb was close by.

## Reading
**Bishop Barron**
*Light from Light*

Hans Urs von Balthasar regarded the cross of Jesus as the furthest trajectory of the Incarnation. Following the prompt provided by the famous hymn in the second chapter of Paul's Letter to the Philippians, Balthasar appreciates the Incarnation as a downward movement, from equality with God to identity with the human race: "Though he was in the form of God, [Jesus] did not regard equality with God as something to be exploited, but emptied himself, taking the form of a slave, being born in human likeness" (Phil. 2:6–7). But the descent of the Son of God did not stop with his becoming human, for "being found in human form, he humbled himself and became obedient to the point of death—even death on a cross" (Phil. 2:6–8).

How wonderfully that last phrase sums up the horror of crucifixion. The point is that God went all the way down, as far as he could go in the direction of godforsakenness, taking on pain, sickness, psychological and spiritual distress, even the agony of total isolation from God. He thereby made all of them potentially a route of access to the Father, effectively sanctifying them. Or, if we wish to shift the metaphor, he "conquered" them, robbing them of their power permanently to separate us from God. Or, to put it in the sacrificial context, he took them on in order to take them away.

One might summarize this theology of the cross as follows. The Son of God went to the limits of alienation from God so that even as the worst sinner runs with all of her energy away from the Father, she finds herself running into the arms of the Son. Here we can see the deep soteriological implications of the Trinitarian doctrine. It is only because God can, so to speak, open himself up, become other to himself while remaining one in essence, that he can embrace all of sin, even the most thoroughgoing rebellion. This is the condition for the possibility of the victorious battle of the cross and of the efficacious sacrifice of the cross.

Within sight of the temple, the Crucifixion of Jesus, involving victim and shed blood, was the work of a high priest. The vocation of Adam and hence of all humanity after him is, on the biblical reading, to be priest of creation—that is to say, the one who offers right praise to God on behalf of all creatures. Sin is a compromising of this vocation. Israel was founded as a priestly people, the nation whose praise was to bring all of humanity, in time, back on line. Precisely because of sin, the act of worshiping God had become painful, sacrificial, for it involved, necessarily, a twisting back into shape what had been twisted out of shape. All of this is summed up and brought to full expression in the consummately priestly act of Jesus on the cross, as he gives right praise to the Father, even while bearing the sins of the world.

Pilate's sign, affixed to the cross of Jesus, announcing the crucified one as King of the Jews was, by implication, a declaration that he was King of the world, for this association was basic to the messianic expectation. So the cross is an altar where an offering is made; it is also a throne from which a King reigns. Spreading the news of this kingship was precisely the work of St. Paul, who refers, again and again, to "Jesus the Lord," *Iesous Kyrios*, an intentional play on *Kaiser kyrios* (Caesar is Lord), a common acknowledgment of the authority of the Roman emperor. Like Pilate, Paul announced to the dominant cultures of his time that a new allegiance was owed.

# Reflection

**Edith Stein (St. Teresa Benedicta of the Cross)**
*The Hidden Life*

The arms of the crucified are spread out to draw you to his heart. He wants your life in order to give you his.

*Ave Crux, Spes unica!* [Hail cross, our only hope!]

The world is in flames. . . . But high above all flames towers the cross. They cannot consume it. It is the path from earth to heaven. It will lift one who embraces it in faith, love, and hope into the bosom of the Trinity.

The world is in flames. Are you impelled to put them out? Look at the cross. From the open heart gushes the blood of the Savior. This extinguishes the flames of hell. . . .

You can be at all fronts, wherever there is grief, in the power of the cross. Your compassionate love takes you everywhere, this love from the divine heart. Its precious blood is poured everywhere—soothing, healing, saving.

The eyes of the crucified look down on you—asking, probing. Will you make your covenant with the crucified anew in all seriousness? What will you answer him? "Lord, where shall we go? You have the words of eternal life" (John 6:68).

*Ave Crux, Spes unica!*

# Prayer

**St. Ignatius of Loyola**
**"Soul of Christ"**
**(translated by St. John Henry Newman)**

Soul of Christ, be my sanctification;
Body of Christ, be my salvation;
Blood of Christ, fill all my veins;
Water of Christ's side, wash out my stains;
Passion of Christ, my comfort be;
O good Jesus, listen to me;
In thy wounds I fain would hide,
Never to be parted from thy side;
Guard me, should the foe assail me;
Call me when my life shall fail me;
Bid me come to thee above,
With thy saints to sing thy love.
World without end. Amen.

# Hymn

*Salve Caput Cruentatum*

**Latin (original poem)**

*Salve, caput cruentatum,*
*Totum spinis coronatum,*
*Conquassatum, vulneratum,*
*Arundine verberatum*
*Facie sputis illita,*


*Salve, cuius dulcis vultus,*
*Immutatus et incultus*
*Immutavit suum florem*
*Totus versus in pallorem*
*Quem caeli tremit curia.*

## English (popular hymn)

O sacred head! now wounded,
With grief and shame weighed down,
Now scornfully surrounded
With thorns, thy only crown;
O sacred head! what glory,
What bliss, till now was thine!
Yet, though despised and gory,
I joy to call thee mine.

O noblest brow, and dearest!
In other days the world
All feared when thou appearedst:
What shame on thee is hurled!
How art thou pale with anguish,
With sore abuse and scorn;
How does that visage languish,
Which once was bright as morn!

Omnis vigor atque viror
Hinc recessit, non admiror,
Mors apparet in aspectu,
Totus pendens in defectu,
Attritus aegra macie.


Sic affectus, sic despectus
Propter me sic interfectus,
Peccatori tam indigno
Cum amoris intersigno
Appare clara facie.


In hac tua passione
Me agnosce, Pastor bone,
Cujus sumpsi mel ex ore,
Haustum lactis cum dulcore
Prae omnibus deliciis.

The blushes late residing
Upon that holy cheek
The roses once abiding
Upon those lips so meek,
Alas! they have departed;
Wan Death has rifled all!
For weak and broken-hearted,
I see thy body fall.

What thou, my Lord, hast suffered,
Was all for sinners' gain:
Mine, mine, was the transgression,
But thine the deadly pain.
Lo! here I fall, my Savior:
'Tis I deserve thy place;
Look on me with thy favor,
Vouchsafe to me thy grace.

Receive me, my Redeemer:
My Shepherd, make me thine;
Of every good the fountain,
Thou art the spring of mine.
Thy lips with love distilling,
And milk of truth sincere,
With heaven's bliss are filling
The soul that trembles here.

*Non me reum asperneris,*
*Nec indignum dedigneris;*
*Morte tibi jam vicina*
*Tuum caput hic inclina,*
*In meis pausa brachiis.*


*Tuae sanctae passioni*
*Me gauderem interponi,*
*In hac cruce tecum mori*
*Praesta crucis amatori,*
*Sub cruce tua moriar.*


*Morti tuae tam amarae*
*Grates ago, Iesu care,*
*Qui es clemens, pie Deus,*
*Fac quod petit tuus reus,*
*Ut absque te non finiar.*

Beside thee, Lord, I've taken
My place—forbid me not!
Hence will I ne'er be shaken,
Though thou to death be brought.
If pain's last paleness hold thee,
In agony opprest,
Then, then, will I enfold thee
Within this arm and breast!

The joy can ne'er be spoken,
Above all joys beside,
When in thy body broken
I thus with safety hide.
My Lord of Life, desiring
Thy glory now to see,
Beside the cross expiring,
I'd breathe my soul to thee.

What language shall I borrow
To thank thee, dearest Friend,
For this, thy dying sorrow,
Thy pity without end!
O make me thine for ever;
And should I fainting be,
Lord, let me never, never
Outlive my love to thee.

*Dum me mori est necesse,*
*Noli mihi tunc deesse;*
*In tremenda mortis hora*
*Veni, Iesu, absque mora,*
*Tuere me et libera.*

*Cum me jubes emigrare,*
*Iesu care, tunc appare;*
*O amator amplectende,*
*Temet ipsum tunc ostende*
*In cruce salutifera.*

And when I am departing,
O part not thou from me!
When mortal pangs are darting,
Come, Lord, and set me free!
And when my heart must languish
Amidst the final throe,
Release me from mine anguish
By thine own pain and woe!

Be near me when I'm dying,
Oh! show thy cross to me;
And for my succor flying,
Come, Lord, and set me free!
These eyes new faith receiving
From Jesus shall not move;
For he, who dies believing,
Dies safely through thy love.

# Reflection

**St. Thomas Aquinas**
**Conference**

Why did the Son of God have to suffer for us? There was a great need, and it can be considered in a twofold way: in the first place, as a remedy for sin, and secondly, as an example of how to act.

It is a remedy, for, in the face of all the evils which we incur on account of our sins, we have found relief through the Passion of Christ. Yet, it is no less an example, for the Passion of Christ completely suffices to fashion our lives. Whoever wishes to live perfectly should do nothing but disdain what Christ disdained on the cross and desire what he desired, for the cross exemplifies every virtue.

If you seek the example of love: "Greater love than this no man has, than to lay down his life for his friends" (John 15:13). Such a man was Christ on the cross. And if he gave his life for us, then it should not be difficult to bear whatever hardships arise for his sake.

If you seek patience, you will find no better example than the cross. Great patience occurs in two ways: either when one patiently suffers much, or when one suffers things which one is able to avoid and yet does not avoid. Christ endured much on the cross, and did so patiently, "because when he suffered he did not threaten; he was led like a sheep to the slaughter and he did not open his mouth" (Isa. 53:7). Therefore Christ's patience on the cross was great. "In patience let us run for the prize set before us, looking upon Jesus, the author and perfecter of our faith who, for the joy set before him, bore his cross and despised the shame" (Heb. 12:2).

If you seek an example of humility, look upon the crucified one, for God wished to be judged by Pontius Pilate and to die.

If you seek an example of obedience, follow him who became obedient to the Father even unto death. "For just as by the disobedience of one man, namely, Adam, many were made sinners, so by the obedience of one man, many were made righteous" (Rom. 5:19).

If you seek an example of despising earthly things, follow him who is the "King of kings and the Lord of lords" (1 Tim. 5:16), "in whom are hidden all the treasures of wisdom and knowledge" (Col. 2:3). Upon the cross he was stripped, mocked, spat upon, struck, crowned with thorns, and given only vinegar and gall to drink.

Do not be attached, therefore, to clothing and riches, because "they divided my garments among themselves" (Matt. 27:35; cf. Ps. 22:18). Nor to honors, for he experienced harsh words and scourgings. Nor to greatness of rank, for "weaving a crown of thorns they placed it on my head" (Matt. 27:29). Nor to anything delightful, for "in my thirst they gave me vinegar to drink" (Ps. 69:21; cf. Matt. 27:48).

# Poem

**St. Teresa of Avila**
**"The Way of the Cross"**

*Within the cross is life*
*And consolation.*
*It alone is the road*
*Leading to heaven.*

The Lord of heaven and earth
Is on the cross.
On it, too, delight in peace.
Though war may rage,
It banishes all evil
Dwelling here on earth.
*It alone is the road*
*Leading to heaven.*

From the cross the bride
To her Beloved says
This is a precious palm
Upon which she has climbed,
Its fruit tasting
Like the God of paradise:
*It alone is the road*
*Leading to heaven.*

This cross is the verdant tree
Desired by the bride.
In its cool shade
Now she is resting,
Delighting in her Beloved,
Heaven's King:
*It alone is the road*
*Leading to heaven.*

The soul to God
Is wholly surrendered,
From all the world
Now truly free,
The cross is at last
Her "Tree of Life" and consolation:
*It alone is the road*
*Leading to heaven.*

After our Savior
Upon the cross placed Himself,
Now in this cross is
Both glory and honor.
In suffering pain
There is life and comfort,
*And the safest road*
*Leading to heaven.*

# Prayer
**St. Thérèse of Lisieux**
**From the Act of Oblation to Merciful Love**

O My God! Most Blessed Trinity, I desire to *Love* you and make you *Loved*, to work for the glory of Holy Church by saving souls on earth and liberating those suffering in purgatory. I desire to accomplish your will perfectly and to reach the degree of glory you have prepared for me in your Kingdom. I desire, in a word, to be a saint, but I feel my helplessness and I beg you, O my God! to be yourself my *Sanctity*!

Since you loved me so much as to give me your only Son as my Savior and my Spouse, the infinite treasures of his merits are mine. I offer them to you with gladness, begging you to look upon me only in the Face of Jesus and in his heart burning with *Love*. . . .

I thank you, O my God! for all the graces you have granted me, especially the grace of making me pass through the crucible of suffering. It is with joy I shall contemplate you on the Last Day carrying the scepter of your cross. Since you deigned to give me a share in this very precious cross, I hope in heaven to resemble you and to see shining in my glorified body the sacred stigmata of your Passion.

After earth's Exile, I hope to go and enjoy you in the Fatherland, but I do not want to lay up merits for heaven.

I want to work for your *Love alone* with the one purpose of pleasing you, consoling your Sacred Heart, and saving souls who will love you eternally.

In the evening of this life, I shall appear before you with empty hands, for I do not ask you, Lord, to count my works. All our justice is stained in your eyes. I wish, then, to be clothed in your own *Justice* and to receive from your *Love* the eternal possession of *yourself.* I want no other *Throne*, no other *Crown* but *you,* my *Beloved*!

Amen.

"In the cross, and him who hung upon it, all things meet; all things subserve it, all things need it. It is their center and their interpretation. For he was lifted up upon it, that he might draw all men and all things unto him."

—ST. JOHN HENRY NEWMAN

Holy Saturday

# THE DESCENT
# INTO HELL

# Scripture
**1 Peter 3:17–22**

It is better to suffer for doing good, if that be the will of God, than for doing evil.

For Christ also suffered for sins once, the righteous for the sake of the unrighteous, that he might lead you to God. Put to death in the flesh, he was brought to life in the Spirit. In it he also went to preach to the spirits in prison, who had once been disobedient while God patiently waited in the days of Noah during the building of the ark, in which a few persons, eight in all, were saved through water. This prefigured baptism, which saves you now. It is not a removal of dirt from the body but an appeal to God for a clear conscience, through the resurrection of Jesus Christ, who has gone into heaven and is at the right hand of God, with angels, authorities, and powers subject to him.

# Reading

**Bishop Barron**

*Light from Light*

Though the Nicene Creed simply says "and was buried," the Apostles' Creed, after mentioning his burial, says of the dead Jesus that he "descended into hell." There are, most likely, two biblical references that stand behind this claim. The first is the assertion, expressed in numerous places in the Old Testament, that the dead go to a shadowy underworld called *Sheol*. This is not a place of heavenly refreshment or spiritual fulfillment; it is instead a dismal and dissatisfying realm, where shades of human beings live a sort of half-life, cut off from community and, most painfully, the praise of God. A particularly telling description of *Sheol* can be found in Psalm 88: "I am counted among those who go down to the Pit; I am like those who have no help, like those forsaken among the dead, like the slain that lie in the grave, like those whom you remember no more, for they are cut off from your hand" (Ps. 88:4–5). Jesus' descent into hell means that he has entered into solidarity with those at the furthest possible remove from the mercy of God. Though it is odd to say, it coheres with a Trinitarian logic: God goes to those cut off from God and overcomes thereby a separation that could never be overcome from the human side.

And this brings us to the second scriptural inspiration behind the doctrine of Christ's descent into hell—namely, 1 Peter 3:18–19: "He was put to death in the flesh, but made alive in the spirit, in which also he went and made a proclamation to the spirits in prison, who in former times did not obey." The prison in question here is undoubtedly *Sheol*, and the prisoners are those dead who, in their lifetimes, had wandered from the path of God. That Jesus preached the Gospel, or better, revealed it in his very person, to these long-forgotten people, is a source of tremendous consolation. How else could we possibly claim the possibility of salvation for those who had lived and died before the saving event of the Incarnation? This passage helps us see that what happened in Jesus, since it was grounded in a properly divine subject, has a ramification across all of space and time.

Might we follow the prompts of *Lumen Gentium*, one of the most striking of the documents of the Second Vatican Council, and speak of the possibility that non-Christians, even nonbelievers, across the ages, *can* be saved? If they are, *Lumen Gentium* argues, they are saved through some participation in the grace of Christ, some light that comes from Jesus, though they might not be aware of it. In the case of nonbelievers, it would happen through following, honestly and courageously, the dictates of the conscience, which John Henry Newman helpfully described as the "aboriginal Vicar of Christ" in the soul. The great English master was anticipating the teaching of Vatican II by insisting that the voice of conscience is, in point of fact, the voice of Christ, though anonymously so. If Jesus were but one spiritual teacher among many, this would not hold, but since he is, in person, the very Word of the Father, the dictate of conscience *is* his dictate. Thus, the "being dead" of the Son of God is not a desperate state of affairs, but rather the ground of our most extravagant hope.

# Reflection
### From an Ancient Homily on Holy Saturday

Something strange is happening—there is a great silence on earth today, a great silence and stillness. The whole earth keeps silence because the King is asleep. The earth trembled and is still because God has fallen asleep in the flesh and he has raised up all who have slept ever since the world began. God has died in the flesh and hell trembles with fear.

He has gone to search for our first parent, as for a lost sheep. Greatly desiring to visit those who live in darkness and in the shadow of death, he has gone to free from sorrow the captives Adam and Eve, he who is both God and the son of Eve. The Lord approached them bearing the cross, the weapon that had won him the victory. At the sight of him Adam, the first man he had created, struck his breast in terror and cried out to everyone: "My Lord be with you all." Christ answered him: "And with your spirit." He took him by the hand and raised him up, saying: "Awake, O sleeper, and rise from the dead, and Christ will give you light."

"I am your God, who for your sake have become your son. Out of love for you and for your descendants I now by my own authority command all who are held in bondage to come forth, all who are in darkness to be enlightened, all who are sleeping to arise. I order you, O sleeper, to awake.

I did not create you to be held a prisoner in hell. Rise from the dead, for I am the life of the dead. Rise up, work of my hands, you who were created in my image. Rise, let us leave this place, for you are in me and I am in you; together we form only one person and we cannot be separated.

"For your sake I, your God, became your son; I, the Lord, took the form of a slave; I, whose home is above the heavens, descended to the earth and beneath the earth. For your sake, for the sake of man, I became like a man without help, free among the dead. For the sake of you, who left a garden, I was betrayed to the Jews in a garden, and I was crucified in a garden.

"See on my face the spittle I received in order to restore to you the life I once breathed into you. See there the marks of the blows I received in order to refashion your warped nature in my image. On my back see the marks of the scourging I endured to remove the burden of sin that weighs upon your back. See my hands, nailed firmly to a tree, for you who once wickedly stretched out your hand to a tree.

"I slept on the cross and a sword pierced my side for you who slept in paradise and brought forth Eve from your side. My side has healed the pain in yours. My sleep will rouse you from your sleep in hell. The sword that pierced me has sheathed the sword that was turned against you.

"Rise, let us leave this place. The enemy led you out of the earthly paradise. I will not restore you to that paradise, but I will enthrone you in heaven. I forbade you the tree that was only a symbol of life, but see, I who am life itself am now one with you. I appointed cherubim to guard you as slaves are guarded, but now I make them worship you as God. The throne formed by cherubim awaits you, its bearers swift and eager. The bridal chamber is adorned, the banquet is ready, the eternal dwelling places are prepared, the treasure houses of all good things lie open. The kingdom of heaven has been prepared for you from all eternity."

# Prayer

**St. Gregory of Narek**
*Speaking with God from the Depths of the Heart*

You alone are God in heaven, exalted and benevolent,
yours is the power, and yours, forgiveness.
Yours is healing and yours, abundance.
Yours are the gifts and yours alone grace.
Yours atonement and yours protection.
Yours is creation beyond knowing.
Yours are arts beyond discovery.
Yours are bounds beyond measure.
You are the beginning and you are the end.
Since the light of your mercy is never obscured
by the darkness of anger,
you are not subject to disease in any form.
You are too lofty for words, an image beyond depiction,
a quantity beyond weighing,
the breadth of whose glory is unbounded,
the reach of whose incisive power is indescribable,
the absoluteness of whose supremacy is limitless,
the compassion of whose good works is unflagging.

You turned, according to the Prophet,
the shadow of death into dawn.
You willingly descended into Tartarus,

the prison of those detained below,
where even the door of prayer was sealed
to free the captive and damned souls
with the commanding sword of
your victorious word.

You cut the bindings of wretched death
and dispelled the suspicion of sin.
Turn toward me, trembling in the confines
of my squalid cell, fettered by sin,
mortally wounded by the troublemaker's arrows.

Remember me, Lord of all, benefactor,
light in the darkness, treasure of blessing,
merciful, compassionate, kind, mighty,
powerful beyond telling, understanding, or words,
equal to all crises, you who are, in the words
of Jacob, always ready to do the impossible.
O fire that clears away sin's underbrush,
blazing ray that illumines every
great mystery, remember me, blessed one,
with mercy rather than legalisms,
with forbearance rather than vengeance,
with lenience rather than evidence,
so that you weigh my sins with your kindness
and not with judgment.

For by the first, my burden is light,
but by the second, I am damned forever.

Now, cure me, O kindness,
even as you did the ear of the one
who attacked you.
Take away the whipping winds of death
from this sinner, so that the calm of
your almighty spirit might rest in me.
Unto you all glory, now and forever.
Amen.

# Hymn

*Sicut Cervus*
(From Psalm 42)

**Latin**

*Sicut cervus desiderat*
*ad fontes aquarum,*
*ita desiderat anima mea*
*ad te, Deus.*

*Sitivit anima mea ad Deum*
*fortem vivum:*
*quando veniam et apparebo*
*ante faciem Dei?*

*Fuerunt mihi lacrymae meae panes*
*die ac nocte,*
*dum dicitur mihi quotidie:*
*Ubi est Deus tuus?*

## English

Like the deer that yearns
for running streams,
so my soul is yearning
for you, my God.

My soul is thirsting for God,
the God of my life;
when can I enter and see
the face of God?

My tears have become my bread,
by night, by day,
as I hear it said all the day long:
"Where is your God?"

# Reflection

**Hans Urs von Balthasar**

*Prayer*

The Son "comes down," and in him heaven becomes tangible on earth. "He who sees me sees the Father" (John 14:9). "You will see heaven opened, and the angels of God ascending and descending upon the Son of man" (John 1:51). Mankind's yearning to look into God's dwelling place is satisfied, beyond all imagining, through God's arrival in the house of man to "come and eat with him" (Rev 3:20). This first descent is veiled; nothing else is to be made known in it but the humble love of God, ineffable by nature, which the late medieval mystics used to call God's "poverty," destined to be so important to man that for the time being it would make him forget all his inquisitive attempts to spy out the glories of the world beyond. In Jesus, heaven is no longer an image but a Person. He is the love of God and can be loved in human form, as a Thou, like you and I. And this Thou dies for you and me; when he dies, heaven is dead to us all. To contemplate Holy Saturday is to contemplate the collapse of heaven into the horrors of the nether world.

But the Son rises from the dead, and the forty days he spends with us establish the fundamental sense of Christian existence: our beloved God, who became man, who became "heaven on earth," who thus wooed our love on earth, and whose love we only reciprocated when he had died for our sake—he is now "earth in heaven." For forty days he shows us this earth transformed into heaven, as if to fan our love for him into an even stronger blaze so that suddenly, when he ultimately goes up to heaven to sit at the Father's right hand, he draws up our love with him.

# Poem

**Pope St. John Paul II**
**"Easter Vigil, 1966"**

This is a Night above all nights, when
keeping watch at Your grave
we are the Church.
This is the night of strife
when hope and despair do battle within us.
This strife overlays all our past struggles,
filling them all to their depths.
(Do they lose their sense then, or gain it?)
This is the Night, when the earth's ritual attains its beginning.
A thousand years is like one night:
the night keeping watch
at Your grave.

# Prayer

**St. Thérèse of Lisieux**
**From "To the Sacred Heart of Jesus"**

At the holy sepulcher, Mary Magdalene,
Searching for her Jesus, stooped down in tears.
The angels wanted to console her sorrow,
But nothing could calm her grief.
Bright angels, it was not you
Whom this fervent soul came searching for.
She wanted to see the Lord of the Angels,
To take him in her arms, to carry him far away.

Close by the tomb, the last one to stay,
She had come well before dawn.
Her God also came, veiling his light.
Mary could not vanquish him in love!
Showing her at first his Blessed Face,
Soon just one word sprang from his Heart.
Whispering the sweet name of: Mary,
Jesus gave back her peace, her happiness.

O my God, one day, like Mary Magdalene,
I wanted to see you and come close to you.
I looked down over the immense plain
Where I sought the Master and King,

And I cried, seeing the pure wave,
The starry azure, the flower, and the bird:
"Bright nature, if I do not see God,
You are nothing to me but a vast tomb.

"I need a heart burning with tenderness,
Who will be my support forever,
Who loves everything in me, even my weakness . . .
And who never leaves me day or night."
I could find no creature
Who could always love me and never die.
I must have a God who takes on my nature
And becomes my brother and is able to suffer!

Amen.

"Since it was fitting for Christ to die in order to deliver us from death, so it was fitting for him to descend into hell in order to deliver us also from going down into hell.... He remained in hell until the hour of the Resurrection."

— ST. THOMAS AQUINAS

# Easter Sunday

# THE RESURRECTION

# Scripture
## John 20

On the first day of the week, Mary of Magdala came to the tomb early in the morning, while it was still dark, and saw the stone removed from the tomb. So she ran and went to Simon Peter and to the other disciple whom Jesus loved, and told them, "They have taken the Lord from the tomb, and we don't know where they put him." So Peter and the other disciple went out and came to the tomb. They both ran, but the other disciple ran faster than Peter and arrived at the tomb first; he bent down and saw the burial cloths there, but did not go in. When Simon Peter arrived after him, he went into the tomb and saw the burial cloths there, and the cloth that had covered his head, not with the burial cloths but rolled up in a separate place. Then the other disciple also went in, the one who had arrived at the tomb first, and he saw and believed. For they did not yet understand the Scripture that he had to rise from the dead. Then the disciples returned home.

Mary Magdalene stayed outside the tomb weeping. And as she wept, she bent over into the tomb and saw two angels in white sitting there, one at the head and one at the feet where the Body of Jesus had been. And they said to her, "Woman, why are you weeping?" She said to them, "They have taken my Lord, and I don't know where they laid him." When she had said this, she turned around and saw Jesus there, but did not know it was Jesus. Jesus said to her, "Woman, why are you weeping? Whom are you looking for?" She thought it was the gardener and said to him, "Sir, if you carried him away, tell me where you laid him, and I will take him." Jesus said to her, "Mary!" She turned and said to him in Hebrew, "Rabbouni," which means Teacher. Jesus said to her, "Stop holding on to me, for I have not yet ascended to the Father. But go to my brothers and tell them, 'I am going to my Father and your Father, to my God and your God.'" Mary went and announced to the disciples, "I have seen the Lord," and then reported what he had told her.

On the evening of that first day of the week, when the doors were locked, where the disciples were, for fear of the Jews, Jesus came and stood in their midst and said to them, "Peace be with you." When he had said this, he showed them his hands and his side. The disciples rejoiced when they saw the Lord. Jesus said to them again, "Peace be with you. As the Father has sent me, so I send you." And when he had said this, he breathed on them and said to them, "Receive the Holy Spirit. Whose sins you forgive are forgiven them, and whose sins you retain are retained."

Thomas, called Didymus, one of the Twelve, was not with them when Jesus came. So the other disciples said to him, "We have seen the Lord." But he said to them, "Unless I see the mark of the nails in his hands and put my finger into the nailmarks and put my hand into his side, I will not believe."

Now a week later his disciples were again inside and Thomas was with them. Jesus came, although the doors were locked, and stood in their midst and said, "Peace be with you." Then he said to Thomas, "Put your finger here and see my hands, and bring your hand and put it into my side, and do not be unbelieving, but believe." Thomas answered and said to him, "My Lord and my God!" Jesus said to him, "Have you come to believe because you have seen me? Blessed are those who have not seen and have believed."

Now Jesus did many other signs in the presence of his disciples that are not written in this book. But these are written that you may come to believe that Jesus is the Christ, the Son of God, and that through this belief you may have life in his name.

# Reading
**Bishop Barron**
**Article**

The Resurrection of Jesus from the dead is the be-all and the end-all of the Christian faith. If Jesus didn't rise from the dead, all bishops, priests, and Christian ministers should go home and get honest jobs, and all the Christian faithful should leave their churches immediately. As Paul himself put it, "If Christ has not been raised, then our proclamation has been in vain and . . . we are of all people most to be pitied" (1 Cor. 15:14, 19). It's no good, of course, trying to explain the Resurrection away or rationalize it as a myth, a symbol, or an inner subjective experience. None of that does justice to the novelty and sheer strangeness of the biblical message. It comes down finally to this: if Jesus was not raised from death, Christianity is a fraud and a joke; if he did rise from death, then Christianity is the fullness of God's revelation, and Jesus must be the absolute center of our lives. There is no third option.

I want to explore, very briefly, a handful of lessons that follow from the disquieting fact of the Resurrection. First, this world is not it. What I mean is that this world is not all that there is. We live our lives with the reasonable assumption that the natural world as we've come to know it through the sciences and discern it through common sense is the final framework of our lives and activities. Everything (quite literally, everything) takes place within the theater of our ordinary experience. And one of the most powerful and frightening features of the common-sense world is death. Every living thing dies and stays dead. Indeed, everything in the universe, scientists tell us, comes into being and then fades away permanently.

But what if this is not in fact the case? What if the laws of nature are not as iron-clad as we thought? What if death and dissolution did not have the final say? What if, through God's power and according to his providence, a "new heavens and a new earth" (2 Pet. 3:13) were being born? The Resurrection of Jesus from the dead shows as definitively as possible that God is up to something greater than we had imagined or thought possible. And therefore we don't have to live as though death were our master and as though nihilism were the only coherent point of view. After he had encountered the risen Christ, Paul could even taunt death: "Where, O death, is your sting?" (1 Cor. 15:55). In light of the Resurrection, we can, in fact, begin to see this world as a place of gestation, growth, and maturation toward something higher, more permanent, more splendid.

Here's a second lesson derived from the Resurrection: the tyrants know that their time is up. Remember that the cross was Rome's way of asserting its authority. Roman authorities declared that if you run afoul of our system, we will torture you to death in the most excruciating (*ex cruce*, from the cross) way possible and then we will leave your body to waste away and to be devoured by the beasts of the field. The threat of violence is how tyrants up and down the centuries have always asserted their authority. Might makes right. The crucified Jesus appeared to anyone who was witnessing the awful events on Calvary to be one more affirmation of this principle: Caesar always wins in the end. But when Jesus was raised from the dead through the power of the Holy Spirit, the first Christians knew that Caesar's days were numbered. Jesus had taken the worst that the world could throw at him and he returned, alive and triumphant. They knew that the Lord of the world was no longer Caesar, but rather someone whom Caesar had killed but whom God had raised from death. This is why the risen Christ has been the inspiration for resistance movements up and down the centuries. In our own time, we saw how deftly John Paul II wielded the power of the cross in communist Poland. Though he had no nuclear weapons or tanks or mighty armies, John Paul had the power of the Resurrection, and that proved strong enough to bring down one of the most imposing empires in the history of the world. Once again, the faculty lounge interpretation of the Resurrection as a subjective event or a mere symbol is exactly what the tyrants of the world want, for it poses no real threat to them.

The third great lesson of the Resurrection is that the path of salvation has been opened to everyone. Paul told us that Jesus, "though he was in the form of God, did not regard equality with God as something to be exploited, but emptied himself, taking the form of a slave . . . and became obedient to the point of death—even death on a cross" (Phil. 2:6–7). In a word, Jesus went all the way down, journeying into pain, despair, alienation, even godforsakenness. He went as far as you can go away from the Father. Why? In order to reach all of those who had wandered from God. Then, in light of the

Resurrection, the first Christians came to know that, even as we run as fast as we can away from the Father, all the way to godforsakenness, we are running into the arms of the Son. The opening up of the divine life allows everyone free access to the divine mercy. And this is why the Lord himself could say, "And I, when I am lifted up from the earth, will draw all people to myself" (John 12:32) and why Paul could assert in 1 Corinthians, "When all things are subjected to him, then the Son himself will also be subjected to the one who put all things in subjection under him, so that God may be all in all" (1 Cor. 15:28). The Resurrection shows that Christ can gather back to the Father everyone whom he has embraced through his suffering love.

So, on Easter Sunday, let us not domesticate the still stunning and disturbing message of the Resurrection. Rather, let us allow it to unnerve us, change us, set us on fire.

# Reflection

**St. Augustine**
**Sermon**

Where is death? Seek it in Christ, for it exists no longer; but it did exist and now it is dead. O Life, O Death of death! Be of good heart; it will die in us, also. What has taken place in our Head will take place in his members; death will die in us, also. But when? At the end of the world, at the resurrection of the dead in which we believe and concerning which we do not doubt. For "he who believes and is baptized shall be saved." Read the following words, which are calculated to make you fear: "He who does not believe shall be condemned" (Mark 16:16). Therefore, death will die in us; but it will prevail in those who are condemned. Where death will not know death there will be everlasting death, because there will be everlasting torments. In us, however, it will die and it will not exist. Do you wish to understand? I am going to repeat to you a few words of those who are triumphant, that you may have something to think about, something to sing about in your heart, something to hope for with all your heart, something to seek with faith and good works. Hear the words of those who triumph where death will be no more, where death will die in us, too, as in our Head. The Apostle Paul says: "For this corruptible body must put on incorruption, and this mortal body must put on immortality. . . . Then shall come to pass the word that is written, 'Death is swallowed up in victory'" (1 Cor. 15:53–54). I have told you that death will die in us. "Death is swallowed up in victory." That is the death of death. It will be swallowed up so that it will not appear. What do those words "so that it will not appear" mean? So that it will not exist, either within or without. "Death is swallowed up in victory." Let those who triumph rejoice. Let them rejoice and repeat the words which follow: "O death, where is thy victory? O death, where is thy sting?" Where is death? You have captured it, taken possession of it, conquered it, sentenced it, struck and killed it. "O death, where is thy victory? O death, where is thy sting?" Has not my Lord destroyed it? O death, when you embraced my Lord, then you died so far as I am concerned. In this salvation "he shall be saved who believes and is baptized, but he who does not believe shall be condemned." Avoid condemnation; love and hope for eternal salvation.

# Prayer

**St. Thomas Aquinas**
**Prayer for the Attainment of Heaven**

O God of all consolation, you who see in us nothing but your own gifts, I entreat you to give me, at the close of this life, knowledge of the First Truth, and enjoyment of your divine majesty.

Most generous Rewarder, give to my body also the beauty of lightsomeness, responsiveness of flesh to spirit, a quick readiness and delicacy, and the gift of unconquerable strength.

And add to these an overflow of riches, a spate of delights, a confluence of all good things, so that I may rejoice in your consolation above me, in a place of loveliness below me, in the glorification of body and soul within me, in the delight of friends and angels all around me.

Most merciful Father, being with you may my mind attain the enlightenment of wisdom, my desire, the fulfillment of its longing, my courage the praise of triumph.

For where you are is avoidance of all danger, plentitude of dwelling places, harmony of wills.

Where you are is the pleasantness of spring, the radiance of summer, the fecundity of autumn, and the repose of winter.

Give, Lord God, life without death, joy without sorrow, that place where reigns sovereign freedom, free security, secure tranquility, delightful happiness, happy eternity, eternal blessedness, the vision of truth and praise, O God.

Amen.

# Hymn

*O Filii et Filiae*

## Latin

*Alleluia, Alleluia, Alleluia.*

*O filii et filiae,*
*Rex caelestis, Rex gloriae,*
*Morte surrexit hodie, Alleluia.*
*Alleluia, Alleluia, Alleluia.*

*Et mane prima Sabbati,*
*Ad ostium monumenti*
*Accesserunt discipuli, Alleluia.*
*Alleluia, Alleluia, Alleluia.*

*Et Maria Magdalene,*
*Et Iacobi, et Salome,*
*Venerunt corpus ungere, Alleluia.*
*Alleluia, Alleluia, Alleluia.*

## English

Alleluia, Alleluia, Alleluia.

Praise by mortals now be given,
On this day from death hath risen
The King of Glory, King of Heaven, Alleluia.
Alleluia, Alleluia, Alleluia.

The morn of Sabbath scarce did beam,
When to his monument there came
Disciples who ador'd his name, Alleluia.
Alleluia, Alleluia, Alleluia.

There Mary Magdalen anxious stood,
And James, and Salome the good;
His body fain embalm they would, Alleluia.
Alleluia, Alleluia, Alleluia.

In albis sedens angelus
Praedixit mulieribus,
In Galilea est Dominus, Alleluia.
Alleluia, Alleluia, Alleluia.

Et Ioannes apostolus
Cucurrit Petro citius,
Monumento venit prius, Alleluia.
Alleluia, Alleluia, Alleluia.

Discipulis astantibus,
In medio stetit Christus,
Dicens, pax vobis omnibus, Alleluia.
Alleluia, Alleluia, Alleluia.

Ut intellexit Didymus
Quia surrexerat Iesus,
Remansit fere dubius, Alleluia.
Alleluia, Alleluia, Alleluia.

Vide Thoma, vide latus,
Vide pedes, vide manus:
Noli esse incredulus, Alleluia.
Alleluia, Alleluia, Alleluia.

The angel sat in white all rob'd,
And to the women he foretold:
In Galilee you'll see the Lord, Alleluia.
Alleluia, Alleluia, Alleluia.

The message scarce did greet his ear,
Swifter than Peter, John drew near
To the Lord's tomb, with hope, with fear, Alleluia.
Alleluia, Alleluia, Alleluia.

The disciples all assembled were;
Among them Jesus did appear,
His peace he gave, remov'd their fear, Alleluia.
Alleluia, Alleluia, Alleluia.

Thomas believed not, when 'twas said
That Christ had risen from the dead,
Until he saw the wounds that bled, Alleluia.
Alleluia, Alleluia, Alleluia.

My hands, my side, my feet, O see!
Thomas, wounds that bled for thee:
Renounce thine incredulity, Alleluia.
Alleluia, Alleluia, Alleluia.

Quando Thomas vidit Christum
Pedes, manus, latus suum,
Dixit: Tu es Deus meus, Alleluia.
Alleluia, Alleluia, Alleluia.

Beati qui non viderunt,
Et firmiter crediderunt,
Vitam aeternam habebunt, Alleluia.
Alleluia, Alleluia, Alleluia.

In hoc festo sanctissimo
Sit laus et iubilatio:
Benedicamus Domino, Alleluia.
Alleluia, Alleluia, Alleluia.

Ex quibus nos humillimas
Devotas atque debitas
Deo dicamus gratias, Alleluia.
Alleluia, Alleluia, Alleluia.

When Thomas, Jesus had survey'd,
And on his wounds his fingers laid,
Thou art my Lord and God, he said, Alleluia.
Alleluia, Alleluia, Alleluia.

Blessed are they who have not seen,
And yet, whose faith entire hath been,
Them endless joy from pain shall screen, Alleluia.
Alleluia, Alleluia, Alleluia.

On this most solemn feast let's raise
Our hearts to God in hymns of praise,
And bless the Lord in all his ways, Alleluia.
Alleluia, Alleluia, Alleluia.

Our grateful thanks to God let's give,
In humblest manner, whilst we live,
For all the favors we receive, Alleluia.
Alleluia, Alleluia, Alleluia.

# Reflection

**Flannery O'Connor**
*The Habit of Being*

For me it is the virgin birth, the Incarnation, the Resurrection which are the true laws of the flesh and the physical. Death, decay, destruction are the suspension of these laws. I am always astonished at the emphasis the Church puts on the body. It is not the soul she says that will rise but the body, glorified. I have always thought that purity was the most mysterious of the virtues, but it occurs to me that it would never have entered the human consciousness to conceive of purity if we were not to look forward to a resurrection of the body, which will be flesh and spirit united in peace, in the way they were in Christ. The Resurrection of Christ seems the high point in the law of nature.

# Poem

**Gerard Manley Hopkins**
**"Easter"**

Break the box and shed the nard;
Stop not now to count the cost;
Hither bring pearl, opal, sard;
Reck not what the poor have lost;
Upon Christ throw all away:
Know ye, this is Easter Day.

Build His church and deck His shrine,
Empty though it be on earth;
Ye have kept your choicest wine—
Let it flow for heavenly mirth;
Pluck the harp and breathe the horn:
Know ye not 'tis Easter morn?

Gather gladness from the skies;
Take a lesson from the ground;
Flowers do ope their heavenward eyes
And a Spring-time joy have found;
Earth throws Winter's robes away,
Decks herself for Easter Day.

Beauty now for ashes wear,
Perfumes for the garb of woe,
Chaplets for dishevelled hair,
Dances for sad footsteps slow;
Open wide your hearts that they
Let in joy this Easter Day.

Seek God's house in happy throng;
Crowded let His table be;
Mingle praises, prayer, and song,
Singing to the Trinity.
Henceforth let your souls alway
Make each morn an Easter Day.

# Prayer

**St. Thérèse of Lisieux**
**From "Song of Gratitude of Jesus' Fiancée"**

You have hidden me forever in your Face! . . .
I have come to sing the inexpressible grace
Of having suffered . . . of having borne the Cross . . .

For a long time I have drunk from the chalice of tears.
I have shared your cup of sorrows,
And I have understood that suffering has its charms,
That by the Cross we save sinners.

It is by the Cross that my ennobled soul
Has seen a new horizon revealed.
Under the rays of your Blessed Face,
My weak heart has been raised up very high.

My Beloved, your sweet voice calls me:
"Come," you said to me, "already the winter has fled.
A new season is beginning for you.
At last day is taking the place of night."

Amen.

"We are an Easter people and 'Alleluia' is our song."

—POPE ST. JOHN PAUL II

# The Easter Season

# THE JOY OF THE GOSPEL

# Scripture

**Psalm 118**

Give thanks to the LORD, for he is good,

for his mercy endures forever.

Let the house of Israel say,

"His mercy endures forever."

Let the house of Aaron say,

"His mercy endures forever."

Let those who fear the LORD say,

"His mercy endures forever."

In danger I called on the LORD;

the LORD answered me and set me free.

The LORD is with me; I am not afraid;

what can mortals do against me?

The LORD is with me as my helper;

I shall look in triumph on my foes.

It is better to take refuge in the LORD

than to trust in man.

It is better to take refuge in the LORD

than to trust in princes.

All the nations surrounded me;

in the LORD's name I crushed them.

They surrounded me on every side;
>   in the LORD's name I crushed them.
They surrounded me like bees;
>   they blazed like fire among thorns;
>   in the LORD's name I crushed them.
I was hard pressed and was falling,
>   but the LORD helped me.
My strength and my courage is the LORD,
>   and he has been my savior.


The joyful shout of victory
>   in the tents of the just:
"The right hand of the LORD has struck with power;
>   the right hand of the LORD is exalted;
>   the right hand of the LORD has struck with power.
I shall not die, but live,
>   and declare the works of the LORD.
Though the LORD has indeed chastised me,
>   yet he has not delivered me to death.


Open to me the gates of justice;
>   I will enter them and give thanks to the LORD.
This gate is the LORD's;
>   the just shall enter it.
I will give thanks to you, for you have answered me
>   and have been my savior.

The stone which the builders rejected
    has become the cornerstone.
By the LORD has this been done;
    it is wonderful in our eyes.
This is the day the LORD has made;
    let us be glad and rejoice in it.
O LORD, grant salvation!
    O LORD, grant prosperity!

Blessed is he who comes in the name of the LORD;
    we bless you from the house of the LORD.
    The LORD is God, and he has given us light.
Join in procession with leafy branches
    up to the horns of the altar.
You are my God, and I give thanks to you;
    O my God, I extol you.
Give thanks to the LORD, for he is good;
    for his kindness endures forever.

# Reading

**Bishop Barron**

**Article**

An emergency tends to focus one's mind and energies and to clarify one's priorities. If a dangerous fire breaks out in a home, the inhabitants thereof will lay aside their quarrels, postpone their other activities, and together get to the task of putting out the flames. If a nation is invaded by an aggressor, politicians will quickly forget their internal squabbling and put off their legislative programs in order to work together for the shared purpose of repulsing the enemy.

Christianity is grounded in what its earliest proponents called "good news," *euangelion*. There is, therefore, something permanently fresh, startling, and urgent about the Christian faith. It is not a bland spirituality or generic philosophy; it is news about something amazing and unprecedented—namely, that a carpenter from Nazareth, who declared himself the Son of God, has been raised from the dead. This is why there is a "grab you by the lapels" quality about the early Christian witness: the authors of the New Testament are not trading in generalities and abstract principles; they are telling the world about a revolution, an earthquake, an emergency. Jesus is risen from the dead, and therefore he is the King. And because he is the King, your whole life has to be rearranged around him.

This evangelical urgency, which Pope Francis gets in his bones, is the leitmotif of the pope's apostolic exhortation *Evangelii Gaudium* (*The Joy of the Gospel*). He knows that if Catholicism leads with its doctrines, it will devolve into an intellectual debating society, and that if it leads with its moral teaching, it will appear fussy and puritanical. It should lead today as it led two thousand years ago, with the stunning news that Jesus Christ is the Lord, and the joy of that proclamation should be as evident now as it was then. The pope helpfully draws our attention to some of the countless references to joy in the pages of the New Testament: "Rejoice!" is the angel's greeting to Mary (Luke 1:28); in her Magnificat, the Mother of God exults, "My spirit rejoices in God my savior" (Luke 1:47); as a summation of his message and ministry, Jesus declares to his disciples, "I have said these things to you so that my joy may be in you, and that your joy may be complete" (John 15:11); in the Acts of the Apostles, we are told that wherever the disciples went "there was great joy" (Acts 8:8). The pope concludes with a wonderfully understated rhetorical question: "Why should we not also enter into this great stream of joy?" Why not indeed? Displaying his penchant for finding the memorable image, Pope Francis excoriates Christians who have turned "into querulous and disillusioned pessimists, 'sourpusses,'" and whose lives "seem like Lent without Easter."

Once this basic truth is understood, the rest of the Church's life tends to fall more correctly into place. A Church filled with the joy of the Resurrection becomes a band of "missionary disciples," going out to the world with the Good News. Ecclesial structures, liturgical precision, theological clarity, bureaucratic meetings, etc. are accordingly relativized in the measure that they are placed in service of that more fundamental mission. The pope loves the liturgy, but if evangelical proclamation is the urgent need of the Church, "an ostentatious preoccupation with the liturgy" becomes a problem; a Jesuit, the pope loves the life of the mind, but if evangelical proclamation is the central concern of the Church, then a "narcissistic" and "authoritarian" doctrinal fussiness must be eliminated; a man of deep culture, Pope Francis loves the artistic heritage of the Church, but if evangelical proclamation is the fundamental mission, then the Church cannot become "a museum piece."

If there is one thing that bothers Pope Francis above all, it is the endless bickering within the Catholic Church itself: "How many wars take place within the people of God and in our different communities!" Elitists on both the left and the right want to establish a Church of the pure, those who hold all of the right positions on the key issues, and they are none too shy about critiquing, attacking, and excommunicating those who don't agree with them. But the Church is meant to be a countersign to the divisiveness and violence of the world, a place where love, compassion, and mutual understanding hold sway. When we become but an echo of the fallen world, then we are like salt that has lost its savor, and our evangelical persuasiveness is fatally compromised. Again, keep in mind the metaphor of the emergency: when a threat or an opportunity of great moment appears, we ought to lay aside our petty (and even not so petty) differences and make common cause.

Twice in the course of the apostolic exhortation, Pope Francis references the ancient principle *bonum diffusivum sui* (the good is diffusive of itself). When we find something that is good or beautiful or compelling—whether it is a movie, a work of art, a book, or a person—we don't keep it to ourselves. Rather, we are filled with a missionary fervor to share it. This principle applies, par excellence, to our experience of Christ Jesus risen from the dead. We want, with a reckless abandon, to give this supremely good news away. This energy, this compulsion—"Woe to me if I do not proclaim the Gospel!" (1 Cor. 9:16)—is, for Pope Francis, the beating heart of the Church.

# Reflection
### Pope St. John XXIII
### Opening Address to the Council

The whole of history and of life hinges on the person of Jesus Christ. *Either* men anchor themselves on him and his

Church, and thus enjoy the blessings of light and joy, right order and peace; *or* they live their lives apart from him; many positively oppose him, and deliberately exclude themselves from the Church. The result can only be confusion in their lives, bitterness in their relations with one another, and the savage threat of war. . . .

The Church's anxiety to promote and defend truth springs from her conviction that without the assistance of the whole of revealed doctrine man is quite incapable of attaining to that complete and steadfast unanimity which is associated with genuine peace and eternal salvation. For such is God's plan. He "wishes all men to be saved and to come to the knowledge of the truth" (1 Tim. 2:4).

Unhappily, however, the entire Christian family has not as yet fully and perfectly attained to this visible unity in the truth. But the Catholic Church considers it her duty to work actively for the fulfillment of that great mystery of unity for which Christ prayed so earnestly to his heavenly Father on the eve of his great sacrifice. The knowledge that she is so intimately associated with that prayer is for her an occasion of ineffable peace and joy. And why should she not rejoice sincerely when she sees Christ's prayer extending its salvific and ever increasing efficacy even over those who are not of her fold?

# Prayer

**Pope Francis**
*Evangelii Gaudium*

Mary, Virgin and Mother,
you who, moved by the Holy Spirit,
welcomed the word of life
in the depths of your humble faith:
as you gave yourself completely to the Eternal One,
help us to say our own "yes"
to the urgent call, as pressing as ever,
to proclaim the good news of Jesus.

Filled with Christ's presence,
you brought joy to John the Baptist,
making him exult in the womb of his mother.
Brimming over with joy,
you sang of the great things done by God.
Standing at the foot of the cross
with unyielding faith,
you received the joyful comfort of the Resurrection,
and joined the disciples in awaiting the Spirit
so that the evangelizing Church might be born.

Obtain for us now a new ardor born of the Resurrection,
that we may bring to all the Gospel of life

which triumphs over death.
Give us a holy courage to seek new paths,
that the gift of unfading beauty
may reach every man and woman.

Virgin of listening and contemplation,
Mother of love, Bride of the eternal wedding feast,
pray for the Church, whose pure icon you are,
that she may never be closed in on herself
or lose her passion for establishing God's kingdom.

Star of the new evangelization,
help us to bear radiant witness to communion,
service, ardent and generous faith,
justice and love of the poor,
that the joy of the Gospel
may reach to the ends of the earth,
illuminating even the fringes of our world.

Mother of the living Gospel,
wellspring of happiness for God's little ones,
pray for us.

Amen. Alleluia!

# Hymn

*Regina Caeli*

## Latin

*Regina caeli, laetare, alleluia,*
*quia quem meruisti portare, alleluia,*
*resurrexit sicut dixit, alleluia;*
*ora pro nobis Deum, alleluia.*

*Gaude et laetare, Virgo Maria, alleluia.*
*Quia surrexit Dominus vere, alleluia.*

## English

Queen of heaven, rejoice, alleluia.
The Son whom you merited to bear, alleluia,
has risen as he said, alleluia;
pray for us to God, alleluia.

Rejoice and be glad, O Virgin Mary, alleluia!
For the Lord has truly risen, alleluia.

# Reflection

**Pope Francis**
*Evangelii Gaudium*

I invite all Christians, everywhere, at this very moment, to a renewed personal encounter with Jesus Christ, or at least an openness to letting him encounter them; I ask all of you to do this unfailingly each day. No one should think that this invitation is not meant for him or her, since "no one is excluded from the joy brought by the Lord." The Lord does not disappoint those who take this risk; whenever we take a step towards Jesus, we come to realize that he is already there, waiting for us with open arms. Now is the time to say to Jesus: "Lord, I have let myself be deceived; in a thousand ways I have shunned your love, yet here I am once more, to renew my covenant with you. I need you. Save me once again, Lord, take me once more into your redeeming embrace." How good it feels to come back to him whenever we are lost! Let me say this once more: God never tires of forgiving us; we are the ones who tire of seeking his mercy. Christ, who told us to forgive one another "seventy times seven" (Matt. 18:22) has given us his example: he has forgiven us seventy times seven. Time and time again he bears us on his shoulders. No one can strip us of the dignity bestowed upon us by this boundless and unfailing love. With a tenderness which never disappoints, but is always capable of restoring our joy, he makes it possible for us to lift up our heads and to start anew. Let us not flee from the Resurrection of Jesus, let us never give up, come what will. May nothing inspire more than his life, which impels us onwards! . . .

There are Christians whose lives seem like Lent without Easter. I realize of course that joy is not expressed the same way at all times in life, especially at moments of great difficulty. Joy adapts and changes, but it always endures, even as a flicker of light born of our personal certainty that, when everything is said and done, we are infinitely loved. I understand the grief of people who have to endure great suffering, yet slowly but surely we all have to let the joy of faith slowly revive as a quiet yet firm trust, even amid the greatest distress: "My soul is bereft of peace; I have forgotten what happiness is. . . . But this I call to mind, and therefore I have hope: the steadfast love of the Lord never ceases, his mercies never come to an end; they are new every morning. Great is your faithfulness. . . . It is good that one should wait quietly for the salvation of the Lord" (Lam. 3:17, 21–23, 26).

Sometimes we are tempted to find excuses and complain, acting as if we could only be happy if a thousand conditions were met. To some extent this is because our "technological society has succeeded in multiplying occasions of pleasure, yet has found it very difficult to engender joy." I can say that the most beautiful and natural expressions of joy which I have seen in my life were in poor people who had little to hold on to. I also think of the real joy shown by others who, even amid pressing professional obligations, were able to preserve, in detachment and simplicity, a heart full of faith. In their own way, all these instances of joy flow from the infinite love of God, who has revealed himself to us in Jesus Christ. I never tire of repeating those words of Benedict XVI which take us to the very heart of the Gospel: "Being a Christian is not the result of an ethical choice or a lofty idea, but the encounter with an event, a person, which gives life a new horizon and a decisive direction."

Thanks solely to this encounter—or renewed encounter—with God's love, which blossoms into an enriching friendship, we are liberated from our narrowness and self-absorption. We become fully human when we become more than human, when we let God bring us beyond ourselves in order to attain the fullest truth of our being. Here we find the source and inspiration of all our efforts at evangelization. For if we have received the love which restores meaning to our lives, how can we fail to share that love with others?

# Poem

**St. John of the Cross**
**"The Living Flame of Love"**

*Stanzas that the soul recites in the intimate union with God*

O living flame of love
That tenderly wounds my soul
In its deepest center! Since
Now you are not oppressive,
Now Consummate! if it be your will:
Tear through the veil of this sweet encounter!

O sweet cautery,
O delightful wound!
O gentle hand! O delicate touch
That tastes of eternal life
And pays every debt!
In killing you changed death to life.

O lamps of fire!
In whose splendors
The deep caverns of feeling,
Once obscure and blind,
Now give forth, so rarely, so exquisitely,
Both warmth and light to their beloved.

How gently and lovingly
You wake in my heart,
Where in secret you dwell alone;
And in your sweet breathing,
Filled with good and glory,
How tenderly you swell my heart with love.

# Prayer

**St. Thérèse of Lisieux**
*Story of a Soul*

"I have run the way of your commandments when you enlarged my heart" (Ps. 119:32). It is only charity that can expand my heart. O Jesus, since this sweet flame consumes it, I run with joy in the way of your *new* commandment.

Amen.

"I have said these things to you so that my joy may be in you, and that your joy may be complete."

—JOHN 15:11

# Conclusion

Friends, thank you for joining us on this journey. Now that Lent and Easter are over, you might be wondering, what's next? How do I maintain the spiritual momentum? I'd like to suggest a few practical tips.

First, be sure to visit our website, WordOnFire.org, on a regular basis. There you'll find lots of helpful resources, including new articles, videos, blog posts, podcasts, and homilies, all designed to help strengthen your faith and evangelize the culture. The best part is that all of it is free!

In addition to those free resources, I invite you to join the Word on Fire Institute. This is an online hub of deep spiritual and intellectual formation, where you'll journey through courses taught by me and other Fellows. Our goal is to build an army of evangelists, people who have been transformed by Christ and want to bring his light to the world. Learn more and sign up at https://wordonfire.institute.

Finally, the best way to carry on your progress is to commit to at least one new spiritual practice. For instance, you might read through one of the Gospels, one chapter per day; or start praying part of the Liturgy of the Hours; or spend some time with the Blessed Sacrament once a week; or decide to attend one extra Mass each week; or pray one Rosary each day. All of these are simple, straightforward ways to deepen your spiritual life.

Again, thank you from all of us at Word on Fire, and God bless you!

Peace,

*+ Robert Barron*

Bishop Robert Barron

# The Stations of the Cross

## Opening Prayer

In the name of the Father, and of the Son, and of the Holy Spirit.

Amen.

℣. Lord Jesus Christ, Son of God,

℞. Have mercy on me, a sinner.

℣. Lord Jesus Christ, Son of God,

℞. Have mercy on me, a sinner.

℣. Lord Jesus Christ, Son of God,

℞. Have mercy on me, a sinner.

# The First Station
**Jesus Is Condemned to Death**

℣. We adore you, O Christ, and we bless you. *(Genuflect)*
℟. Because by your holy cross you have redeemed the world.
*(Rise)*

**Leader:** Jesus stands before Pontius Pilate, the local representative of Caesar. Pilate, undoubtedly sure of his worldly power and authority, sizes up this criminal, asking: "Are you the King of the Jews?" Jesus responds, "My kingdom is not from this world. . . . For this I came into the world, to testify to the truth." Unimpressed, Pilate asks, "What is truth?" And then he condemns Jesus to death. *(Kneel)*

**All pray:** Lord Jesus, Israel dreamed of a new King who would defeat its enemies and reign over the whole world. You accomplished this through your cross and Resurrection, outmaneuvering the sin of the world and swallowing it up in the divine forgiveness. Help us to give our full allegiance to you each day, rejecting the old reign of violence and power and embracing your reign of nonviolence and love.

**(Optional)**

Our Father, who art in heaven,
hallowed be thy name;
thy kingdom come,
thy will be done
on earth as it is in heaven.
Give us this day our daily bread,
and forgive us our trespasses,
as we forgive those who trespass against us;
and lead us not into temptation,
but deliver us from evil.
Amen.

Hail Mary, full of grace, the Lord is with thee;
blessed art thou among women,
and blessed is the fruit of thy womb, Jesus.
Holy Mary, Mother of God,
pray for us sinners,
now and at the hour of our death.
Amen.

Glory be to the Father, and to the Son, and to the Holy
Spirit; as it was in the beginning, is now, and ever shall be,
world without end.
Amen. *(Rise)*

**All sing:**

*Stabat Mater dolorosa*
*Iuxta Crucem lacrymosa,*
*Dum pendebat Filius.*

At the cross her station keeping,
Stood the mournful Mother weeping,
Close to Jesus to the last.

# The Second Station
**Jesus Takes Up His Cross**

℣. We adore you, O Christ, and we bless you. *(Genuflect)*
℞. Because by your holy cross you have redeemed the world.
*(Rise)*

**Leader:** God the Father sends his Son to the cross—not out of anger, but out of love; not to see him suffer, but to set things right. "For God so loved the world that he gave his only Son, so that everyone who believes in him may not perish but may have eternal life." God the Son willingly takes up that terrible cross—a sacrifice expressive of compassion for us sinners. *(Kneel)*

**All pray:** Lord Jesus, you took up the cross; give us the grace to take up our cross daily and follow you. You lived in self-forgetting love unto death; give us the grace to be such love. You broke open your own heart for us; give us the grace to open our hearts for others.

**(Optional)**

Our Father, Hail Mary, Glory Be

*(Rise)*

**All sing:**

*Cuius animam gementem,*
*Contristatam et dolentem,*
*Pertransivit gladius.*

Through her heart, his sorrow sharing,
All his bitter anguish bearing,
Now at length the sword had passed.

# The Third Station

**Jesus Falls for the First Time**

℣. We adore you, O Christ, and we bless you. *(Genuflect)*
℟. Because by your holy cross you have redeemed the world. *(Rise)*

**Leader:** Jesus—crowned with thorns and already almost drained of blood—is made to carry his cross. As he makes his painful way to Calvary, bearing the burdens of the world's sin, he falls under the tremendous weight. *(Kneel)*

**All pray:** Lord Jesus, we so often see the universe as turning around our egos and needs. Rescue us from the insanity of sin, which brings about spiritual disintegration and death. As you bore our burdens, disempowering them from within, may we actively lower ourselves to bear the burdens of others.

**(Optional)**

Our Father, Hail Mary, Glory Be

*(Rise)*

**All sing:**

*O quam tristis et afflicta*
*Fuit illa benedicta*
*Mater Unigeniti!*

Oh, how sad and sore distressed
Was that Mother highly blest
Of the sole-begotten One!

# The Fourth Station
**Jesus Meets His Blessed Mother**

℣. We adore you, O Christ, and we bless you. *(Genuflect)*

℟. Because by your holy cross you have redeemed the world. *(Rise)*

**Leader:** As he carries the cross, Jesus meets his Blessed Mother, the Virgin Mary. The humble handmaid through whom Christ was born now watches him approach his death, a sword of sorrow piercing her soul. *(Kneel)*

**All pray:** Holy Mary, you followed your son all the way to the cross, where he entrusted us to you as our mother and the privileged channel of his grace. Intercede for us, that we might be drawn into deeper fellowship with him.

**(Optional)**

Our Father, Hail Mary, Glory Be

*(Rise)*

**All sing:**

*Quae moerebat, et dolebat,*
*Pia Mater, dum videbat*
*Nati poenas inclyti.*

Christ above in torment hangs;
She beneath beholds the pangs
Of her dying glorious Son.

# The Fifth Station
**Simon of Cyrene Is Made to Help Jesus Bear the Cross**

℣. We adore you, O Christ, and we bless you. *(Genuflect)*
℞. Because by your holy cross you have redeemed the world.
*(Rise)*

**Leader:** The Romans, not wanting Christ to die before his Crucifixion, press into service Simon of Cyrene. How perilous and dangerous this must have seemed to Simon! But he seizes the moment and helps Jesus with the cross, bearing some of his suffering. *(Kneel)*

**All pray:** Lord Jesus, at the moment of truth, Simon of Cyrene saw that you had need of him—and he responded. Help us, too, to see and respond to your need of us. Even if we are unnoticed or mocked, press us into service to bear you into the world.

**(Optional)**

Our Father, Hail Mary, Glory Be

*(Rise)*

**All sing:**

*Quis est homo qui non fleret,*
*Matrem Christi si videret*
*In tanto supplicio?*

Is there one who would not weep,
Whelmed in miseries so deep
Christ's dear Mother to behold?

# The Sixth Station
**Veronica Wipes the Face of Jesus**

℣. We adore you, O Christ, and we bless you. *(Genuflect)*
℟. Because by your holy cross you have redeemed the world.
*(Rise)*

**Leader:** A woman called Veronica approaches and wipes the blood and sweat from Jesus' face as he continues his way to Calvary. An image of the face of Christ—the divine Word made flesh—is miraculously imprinted on her veil. *(Kneel)*

**All pray:** Lord Jesus, in your Holy Face, we see the ugliness of our sin, which rules out our self-justification. But we also see the face of mercy, which lifts us from our self-reproach. In your agonies, you reveal our agony and take it away. Keep our gaze fixed on yours, and strengthen us in our mission of drawing the whole world toward you.

**(Optional)**

Our Father, Hail Mary, Glory Be

*(Rise)*

**All sing:**

*Quis non posset contristari*
*Christi Matrem contemplari*
*Dolentem cum Filio?*

Can the human heart refrain
From partaking in her pain,
In that Mother's pain untold?

# The Seventh Station
**Jesus Falls for the Second Time**

℣. We adore you, O Christ, and we bless you. *(Genuflect)*
℟. Because by your holy cross you have redeemed the world. *(Rise)*

**Leader:** Under the overwhelming weight of the cross, Jesus falls a second time. Here is the suffering servant prophesied by Isaiah, who is wounded for our transgressions and crushed for our iniquities. By enduring the pain of the cross he indeed bears our sins; by his stripes we are indeed healed. *(Kneel)*

**All pray:** Lord Jesus, you entered into our suffering and thereby sanctified it. Make us not only willing to suffer, but willing to suffer as you did, absorbing violence and hatred through our forgiveness and nonviolence.

**(Optional)**

Our Father, Hail Mary, Glory Be

*(Rise)*

**All sing:**

*Pro peccatis suae gentis*
*Vidit Iesum in tormentis,*
*Et flagellis subditum.*

Bruised, derided, cursed, defiled,
She beheld her tender Child
All with bloody scourges rent.

# The Eighth Station
**Jesus Meets the Women of Jerusalem**

℣. We adore you, O Christ, and we bless you. *(Genuflect)*
℟. Because by your holy cross you have redeemed the world. *(Rise)*

**Leader:** As Jesus is led to Calvary, a great number follow him, including the weeping women of Jerusalem. Jesus turns to them and speaks as judge of the world, saying, "Daughters of Jerusalem, do not weep for me, but weep for yourselves and for your children." *(Kneel)*

**All pray:** Lord Jesus, you are the Savior who shows us the way out of our sin. But you are also the Judge who shows us we are sinners. Your every move, word, and gesture, especially your violent death, constituted God's judgment on the world. Whenever we are tempted to think that all is well with us, direct our gaze to your cross, where our illusions die.

**(Optional)**

Our Father, Hail Mary, Glory Be

*(Rise)*

**All sing:**

*Vidit suum dulcem Natum*
*Moriendo desolatum,*
*Dum emisit spiritum.*

For the sins of his own nation,
Saw him hang in desolation,
Till his Spirit forth he sent.

# The Ninth Station
## Jesus Falls for the Third Time

℣. We adore you, O Christ, and we bless you. *(Genuflect)*

℟. Because by your holy cross you have redeemed the world. *(Rise)*

**Leader:** Jesus continues to bear the terrible weight of the cross—a cross so heavy that it causes him to fall for a third time. Bearing the weight of our sin, and entering into our suffering, Jesus now rises to approach the final enemy to be defeated: death itself. *(Kneel)*

**All pray:** Lord Jesus, at the root of sin is fear, especially fear of death. Thus, you journeyed into the realm of death and, by your sacrifice, twisted it back to life. You conquered death precisely by dying. Keep us from living in a world dominated by death and the fear of death, and help us to remember that death does not have the final word.

**(Optional)**

Our Father, Hail Mary, Glory Be

*(Rise)*

**All sing:**

*Eia Mater, fons amoris,*
*Me sentire vim doloris*
*Fac, ut tecum lugeam.*

O thou Mother! fount of love!
Touch my spirit from above,
Make my heart with thine accord.

# The Tenth Station
## Jesus Is Stripped of His Garments

℣. We adore you, O Christ, and we bless you. *(Genuflect)*
℟. Because by your holy cross you have redeemed the world.
*(Rise)*

**Leader:** The soldiers take Jesus' clothes and divide them into four shares, a share for each soldier, and cast lots for his tunic, fulfilling the words of the Psalm: "They divide my clothes among themselves, and for my clothing they cast lots." Christ is stripped of everything: reputation, comfort, esteem, food, drink—even the pathetic clothes on his back. *(Kneel)*

**All pray:** Lord Jesus, on the way of the cross, you despised the addictions of wealth, pleasure, power, and honor, and you loved the will of your Father. You were stripped naked, utterly detached from worldly goods. You went into the furthest reaches of godforsakenness in order to bring the divine love even to that darkest place. Grant that we may despise what you despised, and love what you loved.

**(Optional)**

Our Father, Hail Mary, Glory Be

*(Rise)*

**All sing:**

*Fac, ut ardeat cor meum*
*In amando Christum Deum*
*Ut sibi complaceam.*

Make me feel as thou hast felt;
Make my soul to glow and melt
With the love of Christ my Lord.

# The Eleventh Station
**Jesus Is Crucified**

℣. We adore you, O Christ, and we bless you. *(Genuflect)*
℟. Because by your holy cross you have redeemed the world. *(Rise)*

**Leader:** Jesus is crucified between two criminals, saying, "Father, forgive them; for they do not know what they are doing." Dying on a Roman instrument of torture, undergoing excruciating pain, he allows the full force of the world's hatred and dysfunction to wash over him, to spend itself on him. And he responds not with violence or resentment, but with forgiveness. *(Kneel)*

**All pray:** Lord Jesus, in your Crucifixion, you took away the sin of the world, swallowing it up in the divine mercy. Through your perfect sacrifice as high priest, eternal life has been made available to the whole of humanity. Stir up your Church to deepen its participation in this eternal act through the Mass, where we unite our sacrifices with yours.

**(Optional)**

Our Father, Hail Mary, Glory Be

*(Rise)*

**All sing:**

*Sancta Mater, istud agas,*
*Crucifixi fige plagas*
*Cordi meo valide.*

Holy Mother! pierce me through;
In my heart each wound renew
Of my Savior crucified.

# The Twelfth Station

**Jesus Dies on the Cross**

℣. We adore you, O Christ, and we bless you. *(Genuflect)*
℟. Because by your holy cross you have redeemed the world.
*(Rise)*

**Leader:** From the cross, Jesus says "Consummatum est"—
"It is finished." The work of the Lord has been brought to
fulfillment. He gives out a loud cry, and breathes his last.
Above the crucified God hangs a sign placed by Pontius
Pilate and written out in Hebrew, Greek, and Latin: "Jesus
of Nazareth, the King of the Jews." *(Kneel)*

**All pray:** Lord Jesus, you are the new David, the one who
fulfills salvation history and finally rescues humanity. Help
us to announce the message that Pilate first announced
unwittingly, the message that every person was born to
hear: that you are the new King.

**(Optional)**

Our Father, Hail Mary, Glory Be

*(Rise)*

**All sing:**

*Tui Nati vulnerati,*
*Tam dignati pro me pati,*
*Poenas mecum divide.*

Let me share with thee his pain,
Who for all my sins was slain,
Who for me in torments died.

# The Thirteenth Station

**Jesus Is Taken Down from the Cross
and Laid in the Arms of Mary**

℣. We adore you, O Christ, and we bless you. *(Genuflect)*
℟. Because by your holy cross you have redeemed the world.
*(Rise)*

**Leader:** After the Crucifixion, Jesus is taken from the cross and laid in the arms of Mary, the definitive Ark of the Covenant, who carried the incarnate Word in her very womb. At his birth, Mary placed Jesus in a manger, where animals eat. Now, at his death, she presents him as food for the life of the world. *(Kneel)*

**All pray:** Lord Jesus, the Blessed Virgin Mary cradled you in her arms. Marked with your blood, she presented your sacrifice to us and for us. In her offering of your body, may we be reminded of the Church's continual offering of your Body in the Eucharist.

**(Optional)**

Our Father, Hail Mary, Glory Be

*(Rise)*

**All sing:**

*Fac me tecum pie flere,*
*Crucifixo condolere,*
*Donec ego vixero.*

Let me mingle tears with thee,
Mourning him who mourned for me,
All the days that I may live.

# The Fourteenth Station
**Jesus Is Laid in the Tomb**

℣. We adore you, O Christ, and we bless you. *(Genuflect)*
℞. Because by your holy cross you have redeemed the world.
*(Rise)*

**Leader:** Joseph of Arimathea, a secret admirer of Jesus, comes courageously to ask for the body of the Lord, and a group of women who had accompanied Jesus from Galilee watch carefully to see where he is buried. His enemies had closed in on him, and most of his intimate friends had fled in fear, but these faithful disciples stay with Jesus until the end. *(Kneel)*

**All pray:** Lord Jesus, make our discipleship as complete and consistent as the women who followed you from Galilee to the grave. You went to the cross because you love your Father's will; let we who love you go to that same bitter end, knowing that the stone of our resting place will, like yours, be one day rolled away. Fill our hearts with the joy of the empty tomb, and make us bold in sharing the Good News of your Resurrection.

**(Optional)**

Our Father, Hail Mary, Glory Be

*(Rise)*

**All sing:**

*Iuxta Crucem tecum stare,*
*Et me tibi sociare*
*In planctu desidero.*

By the cross with thee to stay;
There with thee to weep and pray;
Is all I ask of thee to give.

# Closing Prayer

**From St. Thérèse of Lisieux's Act of Oblation to Merciful Love**

**All pray:** I thank you, O my God, for all the graces you have granted me, especially the grace of making me pass through the crucible of suffering. It is with joy I shall contemplate you on the Last Day carrying the scepter of your cross. Since you deigned to give me a share in this very precious cross, I hope in heaven to resemble you and to see shining in my glorified body the sacred stigmata of your Passion.

Amen.

In the name of the Father, and of the Son, and of the Holy Spirit.

Amen.

# Notes

*Minor style adjustments have occasionally been made on excerpted material for consistency and readability.*

## Ash Wednesday: The Shadow of Death

**Reading**: Robert Barron, "Bubbles, Everything Is Bubbles," Word on Fire, July 31, 2016, https://www.wordonfire.org/videos/sermons/bubbles-everything-is-bubbles/.

**Reflection**: John Paul II, "Lenten Station Presided Over by the Holy Father in the Basilica of St. Sabina on the Aventine Hill," March 17, 1999, vatican.va.

**Prayer**: Francis of Assisi, *Francis and Clare: The Complete Works*, trans. Regis J. Armstrong and Ignatius C. Brady (Mahwah, NJ: Paulist, 1982), 38–39.

**Hymn**: Latin text from *Missale Romanum: Ex Decreto SS. Concilii Tridentini Restitutum Summorum Pontificum Cura Recognitum*, vol. 1 (Vatican City: Typis Polyglottis Vaticanis, 1962), 706. English text from *The Order for Funerals* (The Ordinariate of the Chair of Saint Peter), 46–47, https://ordinariate.net/documents/resources/AC_Order_for_Funerals.pdf.

**Reflection**: Vatican Council II, *Gaudium et Spes* 18, *The Word on Fire Vatican II Collection*, ed. Matthew Levering (Park Ridge, IL: Word on Fire Institute, 2021), 18–19.

**Poem**: Gerard Manley Hopkins, "Spring and Fall," in *Ignatian Collection*, ed. Holly Ordway and Daniel Seseske (Park Ridge, IL: Word on Fire Classics, 2020), 195.

**Prayer**: Thérèse of Lisieux, *Story of a Soul: The Autobiography of St. Thérèse of Lisieux*, trans. John Clarke, 3rd ed. (Park Ridge, IL: Word on Fire Classics, 2022), 273.

**Quote**: Romans 6:23.

# The First Week of Lent: Into the Desert

**Reading**: Robert Barron and Brandon Vogt, "WOF 011: Into the Desert of Lent," *Word on Fire Show* podcast, February 23, 2016, https://www.wordonfire.org/videos/wordonfire-show/episode11/, and Robert Barron, *The Great Story of Israel: Election, Freedom, Holiness* (Park Ridge, IL: Word on Fire, 2022), 31–33, 35, 42.

**Reflection**: Athanasius, *Life of St. Anthony* 51, trans. H. Ellershaw, in Nicene and Post-Nicene Fathers, Second Series, vol. 4, ed. Philip Schaff and Henry Wace (Buffalo, NY: Christian Literature, 1892), newadvent.org.

**Prayer**: *The Desert Fathers: Sayings of the Early Christian Monks*, trans. Benedicta Ward (London: Penguin Books, 2003), 51.

**Hymn**: *The Hymns of the Breviary and Missal*, ed. Matthew Britt (New York: Benziger Brothers, 1922), 258–259.

**Reflection**: *The Wisdom of the Desert: Sayings from the Desert Fathers of the Fourth Century*, trans. Thomas Merton (New York: New Directions, 1970), 22–24.

**Poem**: Thomas Merton, "St. John Baptist," in *The Collected Poems of Thomas Merton* (New York: New Directions, 1980), 124–125.

**Prayer**: Thérèse of Lisieux, *The Poetry of Saint Thérèse of Lisieux*, trans. Donald Kinney (Washington, DC: ICS, 2020), 52.

**Quote**: Mother Teresa, *In the Heart of the World: Thoughts, Stories & Prayers* (Novato, CA: New World Library, 1997), 20–21.

# The Second Week of Lent: Prayer, Fasting, Almsgiving

**Reading**: Robert Barron, *The Strangest Way: Walking the Christian Path* (Park Ridge, IL: Word on Fire Institute, 2021), 55–58, 66-68, 70.

**Reflection**: Augustine, "Sermon 207," *Sermons on the Liturgical Seasons*, trans. Mary Sarah Muldowney (Washington, DC: The Catholic University of America Press, 1959), 91–92.

**Prayer**: Dorothy Day, *The Duty of Delight: The Diaries of Dorothy Day*, ed. Robert Ellsberg (New York: Image Books, 2011), 190.

**Hymn**: *Hymns of the Breviary and Missal*, 117.

**Reflection**: Cyprian of Carthage, *On Works and Alms*, trans. Robert Ernest Wallis, in Ante-Nicene Fathers, vol. 5, ed. Alexander Roberts, James Donaldson, and A. Cleveland Coxe (Buffalo, NY: Christian Literature, 1886), newadvent.org.

**Poem**: Gerard Manley Hopkins, "The Starlight Night," in *Ignatian Collection*, 191.

**Prayer**: Thérèse of Lisieux, *The Prayers of Saint Thérèse of Lisieux*, trans. Aletheia Kane (Washington, DC: ICS, 2020), 86.

**Quote**: Leo the Great, *Sermons*, trans. Charles Lett Feltoe, in Nicene and Post-Nicene Fathers, Second Series, vol. 12, ed. Philip Schaff and Henry Wace (Buffalo, NY: Christian Literature, 1895), newadvent.org.

# The Third Week of Lent: Temptation

**Reading**: Robert Barron, *The Priority of Christ: Toward a Postliberal Catholicism* (Grand Rapids, MI: Brazos, 2007), 98–101, 103–104.

**Reflection**: Fulton J. Sheen, *Life of Christ* (Park Ridge, IL: Word on Fire Classics, 2018), 59–60.

**Prayer**: John Henry Newman, *Meditations and Devotions* (New York: Longmans & Green, 1893), 508–509.

**Hymn**: *Hymns of the Breviary and Missal*, 65–66.

**Reflection**: Bonaventure, *The Tree of Life*, in *Bonaventure: The Soul's Journey into God; The Tree of Life; The Life of St. Francis*, trans. Ewert Cousins (Mahwah, NJ: Paulist), 134.

**Poem**: John Henry Newman, "Temptation," in *Verses on Various Occasions* (London: Longmans, Green, and Co., 1893), 132.

**Prayer**: Thérèse of Lisieux, *Prayers*, 116.

**Quote**: Henri de Lubac, *Paradoxes of Faith* (San Francisco: Ignatius, 1987), 183.

# The Fourth Week of Lent: Repent and Believe

**Reading**: Robert Barron, *And Now I See: A Theology of Transformation* (Park Ridge, IL: Word on Fire Academic), xiv–xv, xvi–xviii.

**Reflection**: Benedict XVI, "General Audience," February 17, 2010, vatican.va.

**Prayer**: Teresa of Avila, *The Collected Works of St. Teresa of Avila*, vol. 1, *The Book of Her Life; Spiritual Testimonies; Soliloquies*, trans. Kieran Kavanaugh and Otilio Rodriguez (Washington, DC: ICS, 2019), 450–451.

**Hymn**: Latin text from *Worship: A Hymnal and Service Book for Roman Catholics* (Chicago: GIA Publications, 2001), no. 414. English text from http://www.chantcd.com/lyrics/hear_us_lord.htm.

**Reflection**: Benedict, *The Rule*, prologue, in *Benedict Collection*, ed. Brandon Vogt (Park Ridge, IL: Word on Fire Classics, 2018), 7–8.

**Poem**: G.K. Chesterton, "The Convert," in *Collected Works of G.K. Chesterton, Vol X: Collected Poetry, Part III* (San Francisco: Ignatius, 2010), 313.

**Prayer**: Thérèse of Lisieux, *Prayers*, 75–76.

**Quote**: Paul VI, *Gaudete in Domino* 5, apostolic exhortation, May 9, 1975, vatican.va.

# The Fifth Week of Lent: The Suffering Servant

**Reading**: Robert Barron, *Light from Light: A Theological Reflection on the Nicene Creed* (Park Ridge, IL: Word on Fire Academic, 2021), 94–96.

**Reflection**: *Catechism of the Catholic Church* 601.

**Prayer**: Thomas à Kempis, *The Imitation of Christ* (Oak Harbor, WA: Logos Research Systems, 1996), 133–134.

**Hymn**: *Hymns of the Breviary and Missal*, 172.

**Reflection**: John Paul II, *Salvifici Doloris* 17, encyclical letter, February 11, 1984, vatican.va.

**Poem**: Teresa of Avila, "For the Profession of Isabel de Los Angeles," in *The Collected Works of St. Teresa of Avila*, vol. 3, *The Book of Her Foundations; Minor Works*, trans. Kieran Kavanaugh and Otilio Rodriguez (Washington, DC: ICS, 1985), 402–404.

**Prayer**: Thérèse of Lisieux, *Story of a Soul*, 214.

**Quote**: René Girard, *I See Satan Fall Like Lightning* (Maryknoll, NY: Orbis Books, 2001), 61.

## Palm Sunday: The Entry into Jerusalem

**Reading**: Robert Barron, *Vibrant Paradoxes: The Both/And of Catholicism* (Skokie, IL: Word on Fire, 2017), 40–43.

**Reflection**: *Catechism of the Catholic Church* 559–560.

**Prayer**: *The Didache or Teaching of the Twelve Apostles*, trans. Francis X. Glimm, in The Apostolic Fathers, vol. 1 (Washington, DC: The Catholic University of America Press, 1947), 179–180.

**Hymn**: *Hymns of the Breviary and Missal*, 139–140.

**Reflection**: Irenaeus, *Against Heresies* 4.11.3, trans. Alexander Roberts and William Rambaut, in Ante-Nicene Fathers, vol. 1, ed. Alexander Roberts, James Donaldson, and A. Cleveland Coxe (Buffalo, NY: Christian Literature, 1885), newadvent.org.

**Poem**: G.K. Chesterton, "The Donkey," in *Collected Works of G.K. Chesterton, Vol X: Collected Poetry, Part I* (San Francisco: Ignatius, 1994), 134.

**Prayer**: Thérèse of Lisieux, *Poetry*, 104.

**Quote**: John Chrysostom, *Homilies on Matthew* 66.1, trans. George Prevost, in Nicene and Post-Nicene Fathers, First Series, vol. 10, ed. Philip Schaff (Buffalo, NY: Christian Literature, 1888), newadvent. org.

# Monday of Holy Week: The Cleansing of the Temple

**Reading**: Barron, *Vibrant Paradoxes*, 224–226.

**Reflection**: Joseph Ratzinger, *Jesus of Nazareth: Part Two: Holy Week: From the Entrance into Jerusalem to the Resurrection*, trans. Philip Whitmore (San Francisco: Ignatius, 2011), 21–23.

**Prayer**: Augustine, *Confessions*, trans. F.J. Sheed, ed. Michael P. Foley (Park Ridge, IL: Word on Fire Classics, 2017), 233–234.

**Hymn**: *Hymns of the Breviary and Missal*, 198.

**Reflection**: Francis, "Angelus," March 8, 2015, vatican.va.

**Poem**: Dante, *Paradise*, Canto 18, trans. Anthony Esolen (New York: Modern Library, 2007), 199.

**Prayer**: Thérèse of Lisieux, *Prayers*, 43.

**Quote**: Edith Stein, *The Collected Works of Edith Stein*, vol. 4, *The Hidden Life: Essays, Meditations, Spiritual Texts*, ed. L. Gelber and Michael Linssen, trans. Waltraut Stein (Washington, DC: ICS, 2014), 9.

# Tuesday of Holy Week: The Hour Has Come

**Reading**: Barron, *Priority of Christ*, 104–105.

**Reflection**: Sheen, *Life of Christ*, 352–353.

**Prayer**: Thomas à Kempis, *The Imitation of Christ* (Oak Harbor, WA: Logos Research Systems, 1996), 203–204.

**Hymn**: *Hymns of the Breviary and Missal*, 123–124.

**Reflection**: Elizabeth of the Trinity, "Letter to her mother, September 1906," quoted in M.M. Philipon, *The Spiritual Doctrine of Sister Elizabeth of the Trinity*, trans. a Benedictine of Stanbrook Abbey (Westminster, MD: Newman, 1951), 120.

**Poem**: Paul Claudel, "Stations of the Cross," trans. Rev. John J. Burke, in *The Ecclesiastical Review* 77 (July–December 1927): 415.

**Prayer**: Thérèse of Lisieux, *Prayers*, 106.

**Quote**: Augustine, *Tractates on the Gospel of John 28–54*, trans. John W. Rettig (Washington, DC: The Catholic University of America Press, 1993), 103.

# Wednesday of Holy Week: The Betrayal

**Reading**: Barron, *And Now I See*, 208–209.

**Reflection**: Origen, *Commentary on Matthew* 78, in Ancient Christian Commentary on Scripture, vol. 1B, *Matthew 14–28*, ed. Manlio Simonetti (Downers Grove, IL: InterVarsity, 2002), 242.

**Prayer**: Catherine of Siena, *Catherine of Siena: The Dialogue*, trans. Suzanne Noffke (Mahwah, NJ: Paulist, 1980), 274–276.

**Hymn**: Latin text from *Biblia Sacra juxta Vulgatam Clementinam* (Bellingham, WA: Ed. electronica, Ps 50:3–21, 2005). English text from *The Liturgy of the Hours*, vol. 2, *Lenten Season, Easter Season* (New York: Catholic Book Publishing Corp., 1976), 1180–1181.

**Reflection**: Jerome, *The Letters of St. Jerome*, trans. W.H. Fremantle, G. Lewis, and W.G. Martley, in Nicene and Post-Nicene Fathers, Second Series, vol. 6, ed. Philip Schaff and Henry Wace (Buffalo, NY: Christian Literature, 1893), newadvent.org.

**Poem**: Thomas Merton, "The Betrayal," in *The Collected Poems of Thomas Merton* (New York: New Directions, 1980), 106.

**Prayer**: Thérèse of Lisieux, *Story of a Soul*, 212.

**Quote**: Gregory Nazianzen, *Select Orations of Saint Gregory Nazianzen*, trans. Charles Gordon Browne and James Edward Swallow, in Nicene and Post-Nicene Fathers, Second Series, vol. 7, ed. Philip Schaff and Henry Wace (Buffalo, NY: Christian Literature, 1894), newadvent.org.

# Holy Thursday: The Last Supper

**Reading**: Robert Barron, *Eucharist* (Park Ridge, IL: Word on Fire Institute, 2021), 65–67.

**Reflection**: Ambrose, *On the Mysteries* 54–55, 58, trans. H. de Romestin, E. de Romestin, and H.T.F. Duckworth, in Nicene and Post-Nicene Fathers, Second Series, vol. 10, ed. Philip Schaff and Henry Wace (Buffalo, NY: Christian Literature, 1896), newadvent.org.

**Prayer**: Alphonsus de Liguori, *Visits to the Most Holy Sacrament and to Most Holy Mary*, trans. Dennis Billy (Notre Dame, IN: Ave Maria, 2007), 60–61.

**Hymn**: Paul Murray, *Aquinas at Prayer: The Bible, Mysticism and Poetry* (London: Bloomsbury, 2013), 191–192.

**Reflection**: Ratzinger, *Jesus of Nazareth: Part Two: Holy Week*, 145, 149.

**Poem**: Gerard Manley Hopkins, "Easter Communion," in *Collected Works*, vol. 3, *Diaries, Journals, & Notebooks* (Oxford: Oxford University Press, 2015), 309–310.

**Prayer**: Thérèse of Lisieux, *Prayers*, 115–116.

**Quote**: Ignatius of Antioch, *The Letters of St. Ignatius of Antioch*, trans. Gerald G. Walsh, in The Apostolic Fathers, vol. 1 (Washington, DC: The Catholic University of America Press, 1947), 111.

# Good Friday: The Passion and Cross

**Reading**: Barron, *Light from Light*, 97–99.

**Reflection**: Stein, *Hidden Life*, 95–96.

**Prayer**: Ignatius of Loyola, "Soul of Christ," trans. John Henry Newman, in *Meditations and Devotions*, 352.

**Hymn**: Latin text from *Sacred Latin Poetry*, selected by Richard Chenevix Trench (London: Kegan Paul, Trench, & Co., 1886), 141–143. English text from *Christ in Song*, selected by Philip Schaff (London: Sampson Low, Son, and Marston, 1870), 143–145.

**Reflection**: *The Liturgy of the Hours*, vol. 3, *Ordinary Time: Weeks 1–17* (New York: Catholic Book Publishing Co., 1976), 1335–1336.

**Poem**: Teresa of Avila, "The Way of the Cross," in *The Book of Her Foundations; Minor Works*, 395–396.

**Prayer**: Thérèse of Lisieux, *Story of a Soul*, 278–279.

**Quote**: John Henry Newman, *Parochial and Plain Sermons* (London: Longmans, Green, and Co., 1920), 177.

# Holy Saturday: The Descent into Hell

**Reading**: Barron, *Light from Light*, 100–102.

**Reflection**: *The Liturgy of the Hours*, vol. 2, *Lenten Season, Easter Season* (New York: Catholic Book Publishing Co., 1976), 496–498.

**Prayer**: Gregory of Narek, "Prayer 16," in *Speaking with God from the Depths of the Heart: The Armenian Prayer Book of St. Gregory of Narek*, trans. Thomas Samuelian (Yerevan, Armenia: Vem Press, 2001), https://www.stgregoryofnarek.am/.

**Hymn**: *The Liturgy of the Hours*, vol. 3, *Ordinary Time Weeks 1–17* (New York: Catholic Book Publishing Corp., 1975), 605–606.

**Reflection**: Hans Urs von Balthasar, *Prayer*, trans. Graham Harrison (San Francisco: Ignatius, 1986), 278–279.

**Poem**: John Paul II, "Easter Vigil, 1966," in *The Place Within: The Poetry of Pope John Paul II*, trans. Jerzy Peterkiewicz (New York: Random House, 1994), 140.

**Prayer**: Thérèse of Lisieux, *Poetry*, 119.

**Quote**: Thomas Aquinas, *Summa theologiae* 3.52.1, 4, trans. Fathers of the English Dominican Province (London: Burns, Oates, and Washbourne, 1920), newadvent.org.

# Easter Sunday: The Resurrection

**Reading**: Robert Barron, "The Disturbing Fact of the Resurrection," Word on Fire, March 24, 2016, https://www.wordonfire.org/articles/barron/the-disturbing-fact-of-the-resurrection/.

**Reflection**: Augustine, *Sermons on the Liturgical Seasons*, trans. Mary Sarah Muldowney (Washington, DC: The Catholic University of America Press, 1959), 221–222.

**Prayer**: Murray, *Aquinas at Prayer*, 67–69.

**Hymn**: *The Ursuline Manual: A Collection of Prayers, Spiritual Exercises, Etc.* (New York: Edward Dunigan and Brother, 1857), 456–458.

**Reflection**: Flannery O'Connor, *The Habit of Being: Letters of Flannery O'Connor* (New York: Farrar, Straus & Giroux, 1979), 100.

**Poem**: Gerard Manley Hopkins, "Easter," in *As Kingfishers Catch Fire: Selected and Annotated Poems of Gerard Manley Hopkins*, ed. Holly Ordway (Elk Grove Village, IL: Word on Fire Institute, 2023).

**Prayer**: Thérèse of Lisieux, *Poetry*, 85.

**Quote**: John Paul II, "Address of His Holiness John Paul II to a Group of African Americans," October 2, 1979, vatican.va.

## The Easter Season: The Joy of the Gospel

**Reading**: Robert Barron, "The Joy of Evangelizing," Word on Fire, December 1, 2013, https://www.wordonfire.org/articles/barron/the-joy-of-evangelizing/.

**Reflection**: John XXIII, "Opening Address to the Council," *Word on Fire Vatican II Collection*, 2, 9–10.

**Prayer**: Francis, *Evangelii Gaudium* 288, encyclical letter, November 24, 2013, vatican.va.

**Hymn**: *The Liturgy of the Hours*, vol. 2, *Lenten Season, Easter Season* (New York: Catholic Book Publishing Corp., 1976), 1648–1649.

**Reflection**: Francis, *Evangelii Gaudium* 3, 6–8.

**Poem**: John of the Cross, "The Living Flame of Love," in *John of the Cross: Selected Writings*, ed. and trans. Kieran Kavanaugh (Mahwah, NJ: Paulist, 1987), 293–294.

**Prayer**: Thérèse of Lisieux, *Story of a Soul*, 226.

**Quote**: John 15:11.

## Stations of the Cross

**Hymn**: *Hymns of the Breviary and Missal*, 132–133.

**Closing Prayer**: Thérèse of Lisieux, *Story of a Soul*, 279.